A COUPLE'S GUIDE TO
RELAXING, REFRESHING, AND DE-STRESSING

UNCOMMON WAYS TO
UNWIND TOGETHER

A COUPLE'S GUIDE TO
RELAXING, REFRESHING, AND DE-STRESSING

52

UNCOMMON WAYS TO
UNWIND TOGETHER

RANDY SOUTHERN

MOODY PUBLISHERS
CHICAGO

Unless otherwise noted, Scripture quotations are taken from the Holy Bible, New International Version®, NIV®. Copyright © 1973, 1978, 1984, 2011 by Biblica, Inc.™ Used by permission of Zondervan. All rights reserved worldwide. www.zondervan.com. The "NIV" and "New International Version" are trademarks registered in the United States Patent and Trademark Office by Biblica, Inc.™

Scripture quotations marked NKJV are taken from the New King James Version. Copyright © 1982 by Thomas Nelson. Used by permission. All rights reserved.

Scripture quotations marked MSG are taken from *THE MESSAGE*, copyright © 1993, 2002, 2018 by Eugene H. Peterson. Used by permission of NavPress. All rights reserved. Represented by Tyndale House Publishers, Inc.

Edited by Kevin P. Emmert
Interior and cover design: Julia Ryan / DesignByJulia.com
Cover images: "5" © Shutterstock/Qba from Poland; "2" © Shutterstock/Roman Siggev; couple in chair Julia Ryan / DesignByJulia.com
Interior images: all chapter spot-illustrations: © Shutterstock/Ron and Joe; third strand icon Julia Ryan

Library of Congress Cataloging-in-Publication Data

Names: Southern, Randy, author.
Title: 52 uncommon ways to unwind together : a couple's guide to relaxing,
   refreshing, and de-stressing / Randy Southern.
Other titles: Fifty-two uncommon ways to unwind together
Description: Chicago : Moody Publishers, 2020. | Includes index. | Summary:
   "Enjoy these fun dates that help you reinvigorate your relationship.
   Whether you're going through a difficult season, your relationship has
   shifted into autopilot, or the everyday stresses of life are wearing you
   out, it's time to boost your relational connection and make fun memories
   with these strategically designed activities that provide opportunities
   to enjoy, de-stress, and unwind. -- Provided by publisher.
Identifiers: LCCN 2019030936 (print) | LCCN 2019030937 (ebook) | ISBN
   9780802419385 (paperback) | ISBN 9780802497970 (ebook)
Subjects: LCSH: Marriage--Religious aspects--Christianity. | Dating (Social
   customs)--Religious aspects--Christianity. | Stress
   (Psychology)--Religious aspects--Christianity.
Classification: LCC BV835 .S75 2020 (print) | LCC BV835 (ebook) | DDC
   248.8/44--dc23
LC record available at https://lccn.loc.gov/2019030936
LC ebook record available at https://lccn.loc.gov/2019030937

Originally delivered by fleets of horse-drawn wagons, the affordable paperbacks from D. L. Moody's publishing house resourced the church and served everyday people. Now, after more than 125 years of publishing and ministry, Moody Publishers' mission remains the same—even if our delivery systems have changed a bit.

Moody Publishers
820 N. LaSalle Boulevard
Chicago, IL 60610

1 3 5 7 9 10 8 6 4 2

Printed in the United States of America

CONTENTS

INTRODUCTION BY GARY CHAPMAN, PAGE 7

INTRODUCTION
BY GARY CHAPMAN

Life together can get busy, stressful, and sometimes just routine. It is not what we intended or wanted—it just happens. If we drift in our relationship, we will likely drift apart. We don't want that to happen, so let's put our oars in the water and row together to our intended goal: an intimate, loving, supportive, enjoyable relationship.

In *52 Uncommon Ways to Unwind Together*, Randy Southern gives us unique yet practical ways to relax, refresh, and renew our relationships. Why 52? Because there are 52 weeks in the year. However, let me be honest: it is not realistic to think that you will participate in one of these "uncommon ways" each week. So set yourself a goal: one every other week, or only one each month. At least you will be moving in the right direction.

This is not a book to simply read. It is a book to be experienced. The book provides ideas. You must make choices and take action steps to implement these "uncommon ways" to unwind and refresh your relationship. What I like about the book is that the suggestions are indeed uncommon. Some of these would never have crossed my mind, but as I read them, I think, *Yes, we can do that. Why didn't I think of that?*

Your personality, physical limitations, or emotional state may lead you to draw back from a few of the ideas. However, I think you will find most of them very doable. Don't draw back because "we've never done that before." That's the whole point! Doing the same things week after week with no diversion can lead to boredom. Routines are good. They help us get the necessary things done effectively. But, we need to intersperse the routine with the uncommon.

There are three things I really like about Randy's approach to unwinding: (1) With each idea there is a quote from Scripture with questions that will lead you into meaningful conversations. (2) Each suggestion incorporates one of the love languages: Words of Affirmation, Gifts, Acts of Service, Quality Time, or Physical Touch. After all, our greatest emotional need is to feel loved. In marriage, nothing is more important than meeting that need. (3) For those who are interested, Randy gives a suggested reading from *The Love Languages Devotional Bible*, which has helped many couples rediscover the practical application of the Bible to daily life.

My hope is that as you try some of these "uncommon ways" of unwinding, you will find them so helpful that you will want to share the book with other couples. Marriages either grow or regress. They never stand still. We all need help in relaxing, de-stressing, and refreshing our marriages. In this book, Randy provides the tools to reach this goal.

WHAT ARE THE FIVE LOVE LANGUAGES?
WHAT IS YOURS?

 WORDS OF AFFIRMATION: Actions don't always speak louder than words. If this is your love language, unsolicited compliments mean the world to you. Hearing the words "I love you" is important—hearing the reasons behind that love sends your spirits skyward.

 QUALITY TIME: Nothing says "I love you" like full, undivided attention. Being there for a person whose love language is Quality Time is critical, but really being there—with the TV off, fork and knife down, and all chores and tasks on standby—makes him or her feel truly special and loved.

 RECEIVING GIFTS: The receiver of gifts thrives on the love, thoughtfulness, and effort behind the gift. If you speak this language, the perfect gift or gesture shows that you are known, you are cared for, and you are prized above whatever was sacrificed to bring the gift to you.

ACTS OF SERVICE: Anything you do to ease the burden of responsibilities weighing on an Acts of Service person will speak volumes. The words he or she most wants to hear: "Let me do that for you."

PHYSICAL TOUCH: A person whose primary language is Physical Touch enjoys hugs, pats on the back, and thoughtful touches on the arm. These can all be ways to show excitement, concern, care, and love.

Visit 5lovelanguages.com to discover your primary love language!

PARTY LIKE IT'S 1999 . . .

. . . or 1989 or 2009 or any other year that means something to your spouse. Maybe it's the year he or she graduated from high school. Maybe it's the year the two of you first met. Whatever the case, make that year the theme of a date night. Everything you do and everything you talk about on your date should have a connection to that year.

1

GOING THE EXTRA MILE

How far you take this idea will depend on the personalities of you and your spouse and the amount of time you have to prepare. At the quick and easy end of the spectrum, you could make a playlist of songs that bring back fun memories of your chosen year. You could dig out yearbooks, photo albums, and other personal memorabilia from that time. You could style your hair and/or makeup as you did then. At the more difficult end of the spectrum, you could try to find vintage clothes and perhaps even a car that fits the bill.

MAKING IT WORK FOR YOU

Embrace your nostalgic side as you celebrate life in 1999—or whatever year you choose. (We'll use "1999" in this chapter for the sake of convenience.) If you still live in the area where you grew up, plan your date around establishments that bring back memories of 1999. Eat at a favorite restaurant from your younger years. Play miniature golf, drive go-karts, or go to a drive-in movie at the same place you used to go in 1999. Cruise around the places you used to hang out. Take a walk in your old neighborhood. Hang out at your old playground. Immerse yourself in memories of 1999.

Another option is to make a group event of it. Invite friends from that era who are still local to join you in your celebration. Give them the parameters of the date and make a party of it. Encourage everyone to show up with fitting decorations, mementos, clothes, hairstyles, and accessories.

Even if your present location has no connection to your younger years, you can still throw a 1999-themed party with your current friends—or you can simply plan a date with your spouse at local establishments that were around in 1999.

Throughout your date, focus your conversation on events and memories from 1999. Talk about what your hopes, dreams, and expectations were. Talk about the things that seemed stressful back then and how they compare to the things that cause you stress today.

 ## SPEAKING THE RIGHT LANGUAGE

If Physical Touch is your spouse's primary love language, choose the year you started dating as the theme of your date. If possible, go back to the place where you first held hands or where you shared your first kiss. Re-create the situations as closely as you can. See if you can recapture those old feelings of nervousness and excitement as you hold hands and kiss again.

WEAVING THE THIRD STRAND

Read together the apostle Paul's words in 1 Corinthians 13:11:

> "When I was a child, I talked like a child, I thought like a child, I reasoned like a child. When I became a man, I put the ways of childhood behind me."

Use the following questions as needed to guide your discussion of the passage. (Please note that the responses in parentheses are merely suggestions, ideas to stimulate your brainstorming and give you something to react to. They should not be viewed as the "correct" answers to the questions.)

▶ What are some of the opinions, beliefs, and attitudes you left behind when you became an adult? (Perhaps you came to recognize that your heroes were real people with real issues like you.)

▶ Which parts of your childhood and teen years were hardest for you to put away? (Perhaps there were habits you had to do away with. Or maybe there were friendships that didn't make it through the transition.)

▶ If you could go back and talk to your younger self in (the year you chose for your date), what would you say?

What advice would you offer? (Do you remember what you were going through at that time in your life? Is there something you think your younger self needed to hear that was never said? If you had been there to allay your younger self, what truth do you know now that you would have shared?)

► If your younger self could talk to you today, what do you think he or she would say? What advice might he or she give about dealing with the stress in your life? (Perhaps you take yourself too seriously, or maybe your priorities aren't what they ought to be.)

► How does God equip us to deal with the increased stress and responsibilities of adulthood? (God is with us at every moment, giving us exactly what we need for every situation as long as we are looking to Him as our source of life. He also brings people into our lives to remind us of the truth of who He is and who He says we are.)

Pray together, praising God for His patience and work in your life—for the ways in which He's equipped you to deal with the stress of adulthood and for the people He's surrounded you with who make life better. Ask Him for His continued guidance and peace as you face new challenges and stressors.

Suggested devotion from *The Love Languages Devotional Bible*, page 102 (Reclaiming Lost Relationships)

A CHAUFFEURED COMMUTE

For many people, the commutes to and from work are among the most stressful parts of the day. If this is true of your spouse, you can offer temporary relief from traffic stress by taking the wheel for a day and letting your spouse ride in comfort to and from work.

2

GOING THE EXTRA MILE

If your work schedule is similar to your spouse's, you'll need to adjust it in order to make this plan work. You may also choose to spend time getting the car ready, cleaning it inside and out, as an actual chauffeur would.

Keep in mind, too, that this is a two-part activity. Your spouse will need a chauffeured ride *home* as well. If you'd care to make a full day of it, you could also make yourself available to drive your spouse back and forth to lunch.

If necessary, you may also want to familiarize yourself with the route and traffic patterns of your spouse's commute. The more comfortable you are behind the wheel, the less stress your spouse will feel as a passenger.

MAKING IT WORK FOR YOU

You don't necessarily have to dress the part (although a chauffeur's hat might be a nice touch), but you should *think* like a chauffeur in making your "client's" comfort and convenience your top priority.

Prepare your spouse's traveling space—whether it's in the back seat or the passenger seat—for the commute. Have a variety of pillows (for the head, neck, and lumbar region) on hand for maximum comfort. Set the thermostat at just the right temperature. Have your spouse's favorite coffee—and perhaps a tasty Danish or some other breakfast treat—within arm's reach.

Set the car stereo to your spouse's favorite station—or create a special playlist for the occasion, loaded with upbeat or mellow tunes, depending on your spouse's preference. Set a mood in the car that's conducive to your spouse's peace of mind. If your spouse prefers to talk in the morning, be prepared with some conversation starters. If your spouse prefers silence, honor his or her wishes.

SPEAKING THE RIGHT LANGUAGE

If your spouse's primary love language is Receiving Gifts, wrap a few small presents for him or her to open on the way to work. Think in terms of things your spouse can use in his or her work space: a framed picture of the two of you, a new coffee mug, a magnet of his or her favorite team's logo, a stress-relief ball, a fidget spinner, or some other novelty item. Look for things that might provide small measures of stress relief during the workday.

WEAVING THE THIRD STRAND

That evening, after your spouse has had time to decompress, spend some time talking about whether it was difficult for your spouse to "give up control" of the morning commute and let someone else take the wheel.

Read together Jeremiah 29:11:

> "'For I know the plans I have for you,' declares the LORD, 'plans to prosper you and not to harm you, plans to give you hope and a future.'"

Though these words were directed originally to the Jewish exiles who had been taken from Jerusalem, they resonate with everyone who places their faith in the Lord.

Use the following questions as needed to guide your discussion of the passage. (Please note that the responses in parentheses are merely suggestions, ideas to stimulate your brainstorming and give you something to react to. They should not be viewed as the "correct" answers to the questions.)

- ► How has God prospered our family and given us hope? (God has brought you and your family through struggles. You've experienced His faithfulness in the past, and that gives you hope for the present and the future.)

- ► Why is it (sometimes) still so difficult to give up control to Him? (We often feel terrified of giving God complete control when we face tenuous circumstances. It's easy to give Him control of something like finances when we feel financially secure. But the moment our security weakens, we pull back finances from God and try to take control ourselves.)

▶ How can we help each other loosen the grip on our lives and trust God to take the wheel? (Trust each other to lovingly hold each other accountable in those areas of your lives where you hold back from entrusting things to God.)

For a deeper dive into the topic, look at the stories of the Old Testament prophets Balaam (Num. 22) and Jonah (Jonah 1–4). Both men tried to take the reins of their lives from God's hands. Balaam steered his donkey straight into the path of an angel with a drawn sword. He escaped being killed only because the animal he was riding had clearer spiritual vision than he did. Jonah chose a route that landed him in the digestive system of a large fish.

Swap stories about times when each of you tried to do what Balaam and Jonah did: take the wheel of your life from God's hands. Talk about the less-than-ideal results you experienced and the hard-earned lessons you learned.

Pray together, thanking God for His patience with your efforts to take control from Him and for His wisdom and loving guidance in helping you prosper and giving you hope.

Suggested devotion from *The Love Languages Devotional Bible*, page 769
(Our Guide)

FIRST IMPRESSIONS

What might have happened if you and your spouse had met at a different time in your lives? Would sparks have flown? Would your chemistry have been apparent right away? Would you have experienced love at first sight? These are the questions you'll answer with this quick and creative adventure.

3

GOING THE EXTRA MILE

You can add an extra dimension to this activity by involving some of your friends—ideally, people who didn't know you when you were young. You'll need to create and print out two full dating profiles, the kind you would find on a legitimate dating site. Make sure, however, that the profiles are anonymous—with no photos, names, or clues that would identify you or your spouse.

Ask your friends to read the profiles—but don't tell them who they belong to—and determine whether the two people seem compatible. Encourage them to go into detail in their analysis and talk about which qualities and characteristics seem to match, and which don't. (Obviously, you'll need to keep a good sense of humor through it all, even if they can find no shred of compatibility.)

MAKING IT WORK FOR YOU

The older you were when you met your spouse, the more effective this activity will be. Try to picture yourselves as you were years before you met each other. What did you look like? What were your hobbies and passions? What were you looking for in someone of the opposite sex?

Once you have a pretty good handle on what you were like, create dating profiles that would have suited you back in the day. You can be as creative or as straightforward as you like. Just make sure that your profiles not only reflect who you were and what you were looking for but also are eye-catching. For example:

> *Looking for someone with natural rhythm, an adventurous spirit, and a killer body? I play percussion in marching band, love to go rock climbing on weekends, and swim competitively. I also love trying new foods and watching old movies.*

> *Han Solo looking for Princess Leia. Seeking someone with a spirit of adventure and a love of geek culture. Gold bikini optional.*

Once you've completed your dating profiles, share them with each other and look for common ground. Would you likely have been interested in each other back then? If so, why? If not, why? (And, if not, make sure you maintain a loving, good-natured, self-deprecating, honest tone as you discuss why not.)

SPEAKING THE RIGHT LANGUAGE

This exercise presents a golden opportunity to do something meaningful for someone whose primary love language is Words of Affirmation. Create a second profile for your spouse—this one, a marriage profile. List and describe the positive qualities you see in your spouse—the characteristics that still attract you and make you feel blessed to be married to him or her.

WEAVING THE THIRD STRAND

Read Lamentations 3:25–26 together:

> "The LORD is good to those whose hope is in him, to the one who seeks him; it is good to wait quietly for the salvation of the LORD."

Use the following questions as needed to guide your discussion of the passage. (Please note that the responses in parentheses are merely suggestions, ideas to stimulate your brainstorming and give you something to react to. They should not be viewed as the "correct" answers to the questions.)

► What happens when you try to rush the Lord's timing? (You discover that your reckoning of the "right time" is faulty. You miss out on His immediate blessings when your focus is on what you don't have yet.)

► Why is it sometimes difficult to wait quietly for the Lord? (When we see Him working in the lives of others, it's tempting to be envious. We may wonder whether we're being "punished" or taught a lesson.)

► How do you see God's timing at work in your relationship? (The sharp edges of your personalities that may have kept you from connecting earlier in your lives got smoothed down by your life experiences, which may have made you more attractive to each other when you finally did connect. You also had a chance to mature and discover what you wanted in a spouse.)

Pray together, thanking God for the perfect timing you see in the timeline of your relationship. Ask Him to give you the wisdom to recognize His timing in other areas of your life and the patience to wait for Him.

Suggested devotion from *The Love Languages Devotional Bible*, page 617 (God Speaks. Listen.)

DANCE WITH ME

It takes two to tango. It also takes two to merengue, fox-trot, and waltz. If you've never learned how to do one of these dances—or if you've ever thought about doing any kind of dance routine—here's your opportunity. Set aside a block of time to learn a dance with your spouse.

4

GOING THE EXTRA MILE

It would be a shame to pour your time and effort into mastering a dance only to have no place to showcase your moves. For that reason, you may want to coordinate this challenge with the wedding of a friend or family member. Give yourself plenty of time before the event to learn the dance and get good at it. And when the day of the wedding reception arrives, you can unleash your routine for all to see, cheer, and marvel at. (Just be careful not to upstage the bride and groom.)

MAKING IT WORK FOR YOU

The first thing you need to do is decide on the kind of dance you want to do. Do you want something fast or slow, something formal or informal? Once you've decided what you're going to do, you can decide *how* you're going to do it. There are many different ways to learn a dance. You can enroll in a dance class for formal instruction. You can ask a friend or family member with dance experience to coach you. You can also find any number of tutorials online.

You'll also need to decide how much time you want to put into the process. There are plenty of short routines you could learn in one session. Others, however, may involve a daily or weekly investment of time.

Maintaining the proper attitude will go a long way toward ensuring success. You want to have fun along the way, of course. But you also want to keep a level of commitment and determination to get better each time you practice. You want to maintain a patient and encouraging spirit toward your spouse. Remember, your ultimate success depends on your ability to move as one.

SPEAKING THE RIGHT LANGUAGE

This adventure will likely be right up the alley of someone whose primary love language is Physical Touch. Make sure that the dance you choose offers plenty of opportunities for cheek-to-cheek closeness. While you're practicing, make sure that you occasionally—and purposefully, though not too obviously—"flub" the portions of the dance that require the most physical contact with your spouse, ensuring that you'll have to keep practicing them over and over and over again.

WEAVING THE THIRD STRAND

Read together the following passages:

▶ 2 Samuel 6:14: "Wearing a linen ephod, David was dancing before the LORD with all his might." The context of the verse is the return of the ark of the covenant to Jerusalem, which was one of the highlights of David's reign.

▶ Ecclesiastes 3:1, 4: "There is a time for everything, and a season for every activity under the heavens: . . . a time to weep and a time to laugh, a time to mourn and a time to dance."

Use the following questions as needed to guide your discussion of the passages. (Please note that the responses in parentheses are merely suggestions, ideas to stimulate your brainstorming and give you something to react to. They should not be viewed as the "correct" answers to the questions.)

▶ Why do you think King David danced? (Dancing was one way he knew to express his joy and gratitude.)

▶ Later in 2 Samuel 6, David's wife criticized him for dancing, because it wasn't a dignified thing for a king to do. Why do the opinions of others tend to inhibit us? (When other people aren't experiencing "a time to dance," they may be envious of people who are. So they target our self-consciousness in order to mute our "dancing.")

► How do you know when it's time to dance? (Any time you recognize God's extraordinary blessings in your life is an opportunity to dance. "Telling the time" is often just a matter of being in the moment and being willing to react to it.)

Pray together, thanking God for His presence in your life throughout the seasons of life. Ask Him to give you the courage and unselfconsciousness to dance as joyously as David did—when it's time.

Suggested devotion from *The Love Languages Devotional Bible*, page 942 (The Barren Seasons)

RIFF YOUR WEDDING VIDEO

"Riffing," which was made popular by the TV show *Mystery Science Theater 3000*, involves adding your own commentary—which is usually funny and a little snarky—to a movie while you watch it. Have fun with your wedding video by supplementing it with a lighthearted commentary.

5

GOING THE EXTRA MILE

Fans of *Mystery Science Theater 3000* ("MST-ies") will tell you that riffing is more fun in a group setting. With that in mind, you might consider inviting some of your closest (and funniest) friends over to help you riff. Make an evening of it. Serve popcorn, Junior Mints, and other theater fare.

Set the right tone for the evening by reminding everyone that the video you're going to watch captures one of the happiest and most important days of your life. Many of the people in it are beloved friends and family members. For those reasons, the comments shouldn't be *too* pointed or snarky.

MAKING IT WORK FOR YOU

You'll likely find plenty of things to chuckle about in your video, whether it's the antics of your flower girl or ring bearer during the wedding processional or the dance moves of a guest at the reception.

Reminisce about the minor snafus and wardrobe malfunctions that seemed like such a big deal at the time. Share some "behind the scenes" stories that you've never shared before. Talk about the different emotions you were experiencing at various times on your big day. At what point were you most nervous? At what point were you most ecstatic?

Celebrate your favorite memories of the day. Talk about the things you worried needlessly about. What things seemed important at the time but turned out to be no big deal? If you had it to do over again, knowing what you know now, what would you do differently?

SPEAKING THE RIGHT LANGUAGE

If Words of Affirmation is the primary love language of your spouse, make sure you do a lot of "anti-riffing" whenever he or she is onscreen. Talk about the excitement and awe you felt when you saw him or her for the first time during the ceremony. You might even rewind certain scenes featuring your spouse just so you can get another glimpse of him or her.

WEAVING THE THIRD STRAND

Read together Ecclesiastes 4:9–12:

"Two are better than one, because they have a good return for their labor: If either of them falls down, one can help the other up. But pity anyone who falls and has no one to help them up. Also, if two lie down together, they will keep warm. But how can one keep warm alone? Though one may be overpowered, two can defend themselves. A cord of three strands is not quickly broken."

Use the following questions as needed to guide your discussion of the passage. (Please note that the responses in parentheses are merely suggestions, ideas to stimulate your brainstorming and give you something to react to. They should not be viewed as the "correct" answers to the questions.)

- ▶ The third cord in a relationship is God. What role does He play in a healthy marriage? (He is woven together with the husband and wife to create a single cord. That means He is present in every aspect of the relationship. He gives it strength and durability.)

- ▶ How does a couple draw strength from God's third cord? How do they incorporate Him in their relationship? (They view their relationship through His lens. They live according to the principles of His Word. They make His priorities their priorities.)

▶ In what areas do you need to draw on God's strength and presence in your relationship? (God's wisdom can be applied to everything from finances to physical intimacy to managing your priorities.)

Pray together, thanking God for His presence in your relationship. Thank Him for the struggles that tested the bonds of your marriage and showed you that those bonds could not be broken.

Suggested devotion from *The Love Languages Devotional Bible*, page 82 (Becoming Covenant Partners)

HOW DO I KISS THEE? LET ME COUNT THE WAYS

Sure, you're both great kissers. No one's questioning that. But are you *creative* kissers? Here's an opportunity to find out. Your challenge is simple: find the most creative locations and ways to kiss your spouse and document the results.

6

GOING THE EXTRA MILE

You can make this adventure even more memorable by recruiting other people to help you pull it off. Put the camera in the hands of your most creative friends and family members—especially those with a photography background. Let them suggest locations, poses, and dramatic lighting techniques that you may not be able to capture on your own.

Encourage your helpers to shoot not just still shots but short video clips as well. That way, you'll be able to create a multimedia presentation—not to mention a few GIFs and memes.

MAKING IT WORK FOR YOU

Here's an adventure with limitless payoff (every time you snap a picture, you get to kiss your spouse) and limitless potential. Let your creativity run wild as you look for interesting locations and scenarios in which to do your kissing. In some photos, you may choose to wear unusual costumes. In others, you may choose to arrange yourselves in unusual positions.

You may choose to re-create memorable kisses from your past—your first kiss, your most awkward kiss, your "You may now kiss the bride" kiss (in approximately the same positions at the altar in the church where you got married, if possible). You may choose to re-create famous kisses from your favorite TV shows and movies (bonus points for re-creating the famous upside-down kiss from *Spider-Man*).

Before you shoot the photos and video clips, think about what you want to do with them. That way, you can play to the camera and give yourself plenty of intriguing shots and clips to use. Think in terms not just of photos but of eye-catching GIFs and memes.

SPEAKING THE RIGHT LANGUAGE

You can take this adventure to the next level if your spouse's primary love language is Acts of Service. After you've taken the photos, curate them in several different ways. Compile them in a slideshow. Create GIFs from video snippets and add romantic and funny captions. Download the entire album of photos on your spouse's computer so he or she can post favorites on social media.

WEAVING THE THIRD STRAND

Read together Song of Songs 1:2–4:

"Let him kiss me with the kisses of his mouth—for your love is more delightful than wine. Pleasing is the fragrance of your perfumes; your name is like perfume poured out. No wonder the young women love you! Take me away with you—let us hurry! Let the king bring me into his chambers."

Use the following questions as needed to guide your discussion of the passage. (Please note that the responses in parentheses are merely suggestions, ideas to stimulate your brainstorming and give you something to react to. They should not be viewed as the "correct" answers to the questions.)

▶ Why do you think God included passages like this in His Word? (He created us to enjoy physical pleasures. The romantic longings and sexual desires that are stirred by our spouses are part of His design. So it makes sense that passages celebrating that design would be found in His Word.)

▶ Why might some people be surprised to find passages like this in the Bible? (They assume that the Bible is an ancient rule book, filled with "Thou shall nots" designed to spoil our fun and pleasure. In reality, the Bible is God's self-revelation of who He is and who He has created us to be. It may be surprising, as it probably doesn't match up with people's stereotypical perception of Christians, but these passages make clear that God created us as passionate people. He gave us sexual desires, and they are good within the framework He has provided.)

▶ How would you reword this passage if you were going to personalize it for your spouse? What words and phrases would you use to describe his or her appearance, kisses, and appeal to you? (The language and images you use are up to you, but this is a place for your best and most romantic effort.)

Pray together, praising God for creating the many attractive qualities in your spouse—and for creating you with such a strong appreciation for those qualities. Thank Him for the unique physical, emotional, mental, and spiritual chemistry of your relationship. Ask Him to bless your efforts to celebrate and enjoy the pleasures of that relationship.

Suggested devotion from *The Love Languages Devotional Bible*, page 739 (Lovers)

ADVISING ROOKIES

What couples did you and your spouse draw inspiration from when you first got together? Who influenced your ideas of what a marriage could be like? Here's a chance for you to serve a similar role in the lives of a young couple. By drawing on your wealth of experience and hard-earned wisdom, you may be able to offer guidance to newlyweds who are just beginning the marriage journey.

7

GOING THE EXTRA MILE

You could go the extra mile in a life-changing way by establishing an ongoing mentoring relationship with a young couple. The relationship can be as formal or as informal as you and the other couple would like it to be. You could get together once a month or so to touch base, to renew your acquaintance, and to offer encouragement and advice. Or you and your spouse could make yourselves available to your young friends as needed, whether it be to serve as a sounding board or to offer ideas.

MAKING IT WORK FOR YOU

Write a card to a newly engaged couple, offering playful, funny, and helpful tips for making their marriage thrive. There are any number of approaches you can take, depending on the circumstances and your relationship with the couple.

You may repeat advice that proved helpful to you. You may offer specific tips for certain aspects of marriage. You may share lessons that you had to learn the hard way—mistakes you made or assumptions you had that turned out to be wrong. The more open and transparent you are, the more of an impact your words will have. Be sure that you phrase everything—even the mistakes and hard-earned lessons—in a positive context. You'll also want to make sure that you cast your spouse in a positive light. Playful jibes are okay, as long as the overall message is a deep and abiding love for your spouse—and gratitude to the Lord for bringing you together.

Sometimes the best thing you can do for a starry-eyed couple is to help them understand that marriage is hard work at times. Obviously, that work is ultimately rewarding, but it's hard nevertheless. By reminding them of that fact, you're preparing them for tough times and giving them assurance that they're not doing anything "wrong" when they struggle. They're simply learning to live with each other, which is a challenge for almost every couple.

SPEAKING THE RIGHT LANGUAGE

While you're reflecting on and sharing your best advice for marriage, you can do something special for a spouse whose primary love language is Receiving Gifts. If you know a local artist or craftsperson who creates signs or plaques, you could commission a wall hanging for your home that summarizes the philosophy of your marriage. Think of a phrase or sentence that encapsulates your relationship and have it artistically rendered in a way that your spouse will like.

WEAVING THE THIRD STRAND

Read together Psalm 145:4:

"One generation commends your works to another;
they tell of your mighty acts."

Read also the apostle Paul's instructions to mature women in Titus 2:3–5 and the apostle Peter's instructions to church elders in 1 Peter 5:1–5.

Use the following questions as needed to guide your discussion of the passages. (Please note that the responses in parentheses are merely suggestions, ideas to stimulate your brainstorming and give you something to react to. They should not be viewed as the "correct" answers to the questions.)

▶ Who can be a mentor? (Being a mentor isn't necessarily a matter of age. Anyone who has relevant experience or godly wisdom can be a mentor.)

► Who are some of the mentors God has brought into your life? Think especially about how they've influenced your marriage and relationships. (Many mentors lead by example. They don't necessarily talk about what they're doing right; they just do it. Think of the aspects of your parents' marriage—or your grandparents' marriage or the marriage of your best friend's parents—that you've incorporated into your own relationship.)

Pray together, thanking God for the mentors He brought into your life. Ask Him to give you the wisdom, compassion, and courage to serve as mentors to others.

Suggested devotion from *The Love Languages Devotional Bible*, page 376 (Taking Advice)

SAND DAY

Sand is used for everything from measuring time to making glass, from holding back floodwaters to absorbing oil spills. Yet one very useful application of sand often gets overlooked—that is, as the theme of a relaxing date with your spouse. You can correct that by planning a day of adventures with your spouse that all have something to do with sand.

8

GOING THE EXTRA MILE

The best way to take this adventure to the next level would be to visit your nearest beach. Because the activities are centered specifically on sand, you don't have to worry about the water temperature. You could have a sand day in any season, weather permitting.

MAKING IT WORK FOR YOU

Your sand-related day may take you in any number of directions. You can fill a sandbox in your backyard, pull your beach chairs close to it, and dip your toes in the sand while you read and enjoy a refreshing beverage.

Better yet, you can build sandcastles in it. You can make sand art together. (Kits can be found in any hobby store or online.) Another option is to attend a glassblowing exhibition. (After all, sand is used to make glass.)

Talk about how sand can be an irritant, especially when it gets in your shoes or swimsuit. However, in oysters, sand is the catalyst for the creation of something beautiful and valuable. When a grain of sand gets inside an oyster shell, the oyster secretes a fluid to coat it with layer after layer of a substance called nacre. The eventual result is the creation of a pearl.

This is a helpful analogy for marriage. When an irritant works its way into your relationship, it can cause discomfort. When you cover that irritant with love, patience, understanding, and grace, you create something beautiful, something lasting, something valuable. You learn to live in harmony with your spouse.

SPEAKING THE RIGHT LANGUAGE

A decorative hourglass would make a great memento of your sandy adventure—and a meaningful expression of love to someone whose primary love language is Receiving Gifts. Another option is to create a memento using sand art and present it to your spouse.

WEAVING THE THIRD STRAND

Read together three passages that talk about sand:

▶ Genesis 22:17: "I will surely bless you and make your descendants as numerous as the stars in the sky and as the sand on the seashore."

- Matthew 7:26: "But everyone who hears these words of mine and does not put them into practice is like a foolish man who built his house on sand."

- Psalm 139:17–18: "How precious to me are your thoughts, God! How vast is the sum of them! Were I to count them, they would outnumber the grains of sand—when I awake, I am still with you."

Use the following questions as needed to guide your discussion of the passages. (Please note that the responses in parentheses are merely suggestions, ideas to stimulate your brainstorming and give you something to react to. They should not be viewed as the "correct" answers to the questions.)

- Look at the passage in Genesis again. How does sand represent God's faithfulness to His promises? (God promised Abraham that his descendants would be as numerous as the sand on the seashore. God waited until Abraham was one hundred years old to begin fulfilling that promise.)

- What comfort and encouragement can we take from that? (Obstacles that seem insurmountable to us, such as Abraham's age, are barely an afterthought to God. Nothing can hinder Him or stand in the way of His accomplishing His will.)

- Look at the passage in Matthew again. What happened when the foolish man built his house on the sand? (The house's foundation wasn't strong enough to withstand storms.)

► What are some things, other than Jesus, that people try to build their lives on? (Some people try to build their lives on pleasure and freedom—doing what they want to do, when they want to do it. Others try to build their lives on false philosophies and religions.)

► The passage in Psalms indicates that there is more evidence of God's wisdom in the world than there are grains of sand. Why is it important for us to recognize and acknowledge God's wisdom? (The more often we acknowledge and celebrate God's wisdom, the more likely we are to turn to Him in times of need.)

Pray together, thanking God for His faithfulness to His promises and for the mountain of evidence testifying to His wisdom. Ask Him to help you test the foundation of your life to make sure that it's built on solid ground.

Suggested devotion from *The Love Languages Devotional Bible*, page 1060 (Honoring Our Parents)

HONEY, TAKE THE LEAD

Here's a definitive answer to the age-old decision-making lament "I don't know, what do *you* want to do?" Surprise your spouse by making every decision and arrangement for a day out (or a day in). Let your spouse relax while you take care of the planning and details.

9

GOING THE EXTRA MILE

The success of this adventure will depend on your ability to make decisions and plans that your spouse will appreciate. A little advance work will go a long way toward crafting a memorable experience. Your best strategy is to listen and take notes on the casual comments and asides your spouse drops when you're together: "I can't wait to see that movie"; "I need a massage"; "We haven't gone hiking in forever"; "The neighbors said that new seafood place is incredible." If your spouse isn't especially chatty on the subject, you may need to do some prodding with a few probing but inconspicuous questions.

MAKING IT WORK FOR YOU

You can take this adventure in a number of different directions. If you go out, you may determine everything—from the time you leave to the outfit your spouse wears to the music you listen to in the car to the topics of conversation at dinner. If you stay in, you may plan dinner, decide which movie to watch as a family, and decide which books to read at bedtime.

Just keep in mind that your aim is to be helpful and not controlling. You want your spouse to feel relief at having the burden of decision-making temporarily lifted.

During your time together, talk a little about how nice it is to take an occasional break from decision-making and other responsibilities and allow someone else to shoulder the burden.

SPEAKING THE RIGHT LANGUAGE

If Acts of Service is the primary love language of your spouse, this activity likely will scratch a deep itch for him or her. You can continue to show love to him or her in a powerful way by repeating the exercise again and again and again. Look for an opportunity every week (or every day, if you're feeling ambitious) to relieve your spouse of a burdensome decision-making responsibility. That may involve anything from planning and preparing an evening meal to negotiating car pool details.

WEAVING THE THIRD STRAND

Read together Galatians 6:2:

"Carry each other's burdens, and in this way you will fulfill the law of Christ."

Use the following questions as needed to guide your discussion of the passage. (Please note that the responses in parentheses are merely suggestions, ideas to stimulate your brainstorming and give you something to react to. They should not be viewed as the "correct" answers to the questions.)

- ▶ How do we carry each other's burdens in our marriage? (You share with each other the good and bad things that are going on in your lives. You give each other "a night off" from the demands of family life and adult responsibilities.)

- ▶ What happens if the burden carrying gets out of balance? (If one person is doing all the "heavy lifting" in the relationship, he or she may get exhausted—if not physically, then emotionally or mentally. In time, that exhaustion may turn into resentment.)

- ▶ How do you know when it's time to carry and when it's time to let your spouse do the carrying? (Talking about it is the obvious answer. And while maintaining an open line of communication is ideal, not everyone is comfortable talking about their struggles and needs. That's why it's important to stay attuned to each other's moods, mindsets, and silent struggles.)

- ▶ Name one way your spouse could carry a burden for you right now. (It may be something as simple as a night off from preparing dinner or something long term, such as a regular time every evening to talk to each other about your struggles and needs.)

Pray together, thanking God for His wisdom and compassion in creating marriage as a relationship in which two people carry each other's burdens. Thank Him for your spouse and the many different ways in which he or she helps you shoulder your responsibilities. Ask Him to give you the wisdom to recognize each other's needs and the courage to speak up when you need your spouse's help.

Suggested devotion from *The Love Languages Devotional Bible*, page 1242 (Bearing Each Other's Burdens)

A TRIP TO THE FARMERS MARKET

The premise may seem a little unusual, but the challenge it presents can be fun and exciting. Here's how it works. You visit a farmers market before breakfast, and the only food you eat the entire day is what you gather there.

10

GOING THE EXTRA MILE

You don't want to set yourself up for failure—not to mention late-day hunger—by visiting an understocked farmers market. Before you embark on this adventure, scout the farmers markets in your area to ensure they offer what you need to subsist for an entire day. If it turns out that you have to visit two or more to get what you need, adjust your plans accordingly. Just make sure that when you leave the last one, you have everything you need for the day.

MAKING IT WORK FOR YOU

Have fun planning and shopping for your meals. Think through your choices carefully. You'll likely want to try some new delicacies. But it might be wise to supplement them with plenty of reliable standbys. You can take the idea as far as you like. If you really want to be strict about it, you could say that *anything* you use for your meal, including spices and condiments, must be purchased at the farmers market.

While you shop, talk about what it would be like to have to gather your food *every* day, knowing that you had nothing in your refrigerator, pantry, or cabinets to fall back on. Talk about the challenges faced by homeless people and others who can't afford to feed themselves or their families.

You might also do an online search of "subsistence farming" in order to discover more about the people around the world who must grow everything they need to survive. Talk about the pressures of relying on the weather, the soil, and other factors that are beyond your control.

SPEAKING THE RIGHT LANGUAGE

If Acts of Service is the primary love language of your spouse, be purposeful in your approach to gathering food at the farmers market. Before you go, find a recipe for a dish (or an entire meal) that you think your spouse would enjoy. Make sure that all the ingredients can be found at the farmers market. Collect what you need and then prepare the meal, giving your spouse a chance to relax.

WEAVING THE THIRD STRAND

Read Exodus 16 together. In the passage, the Hebrew people are in the wilderness, having been led by God, through His servant Moses, out of slavery in Egypt. But the faith of the Hebrew people was weak. Even though God had demonstrated His miraculous power and provision time and time again, they panicked, wondering where they would find food in such a desolate place. Once again, God responded in a miraculous way.

Use the following questions as needed to guide your discussion of the passage. (Please note that the responses in parentheses are merely suggestions, ideas to stimulate your brainstorming and give you something to react to. They should not be viewed as the "correct" answers to the questions.)

► According to Numbers 11:4–10, the Hebrew people eventually started complaining about the manna. What causes people to become dissatisfied with God's provisions? (We start to believe that God "owes" us something. If we don't maintain a fresh sense of awe and gratitude over the fact that the Creator of the universe provides for our needs, we may start to take His provisions for granted.)

► Do you think most people fully appreciate their God-given provisions? Explain. (It's tempting to compare ourselves to people who have more than we do and wonder why God hasn't blessed us with what they have.)

► How can we cultivate a continuously and sincerely grateful attitude toward our God-given provisions? (Changing our focus—measuring ourselves against people who have *less* than we do—can be an eye-opening and attitude-changing experience. It can also turn our attention to people in need.)

Pray together, praising God for His generosity and His provisions in your life. Ask Him to help you recognize those provisions and maintain a fresh sense of gratitude and humility.

Suggested devotion from *The Love Languages Devotional Bible*, page 1314 (Our Provider)

DUAL SUSPENSION

What could be more relaxing than an afternoon spent swaying in the breeze with your loved one, enjoying a good book, the great outdoors, and perhaps a nice, long nap? All you need are two hammocks, four trees, and a little balance and coordination.

11

GOING THE EXTRA MILE

To minimize your preliminaries and maximize your relaxation time, you might want to do a dry run of your hammock adventure. Stake out a secluded spot with the features you're looking for—namely, trees that are close enough for the two of you to recline side by side. Practice securing the hammocks to the trees and then taking them down. (This is an especially good idea if you don't have a lot of experience with hammocks.) Work out all the kinks beforehand so that you can maintain a relaxed, easygoing vibe during your outing with your spouse.

MAKING IT WORK FOR YOU

If you don't have the necessary equipment, you'll find that hammocks can be purchased for cheap—and borrowed for even cheaper. If you know two high schoolers or college students, you probably know two people with hammocks. One of the great things about hammocks is that they can be hung in a variety of places, from your backyard (assuming you have trees) to a local forest preserve to a state park. So you have a lot of options with this activity.

Those options extend to what you *do* in your hammocks. You can read, listen to music, talk, enjoy the sights and sounds of nature, or sleep. More to the point, you can spend time together, relaxing in the quietness and beauty of the great outdoors.

To ensure maximum comfort, you may want to bring along some pillows, sunscreen, and mosquito repellant.

SPEAKING THE RIGHT LANGUAGE

You can make your hammock time especially memorable for your spouse if his or her primary love language is Receiving Gifts. After you set up the hammocks, leave a couple of presents on your spouse's bunk. The first could be a book, something appropriately light for your spouse to read. The second could be your spouse's favorite music device, with a special playlist loaded on it. Create an appropriately relaxing soundtrack for your hammock experience. It would also be good to have a bottle of water and snack for your spouse.

WEAVING THE THIRD STRAND

Read together Psalm 46:10:

"Be still, and know that I am God."

Use the following questions as needed to guide your discussion of the passage. (Please note that the responses in parentheses are merely suggestions, ideas to stimulate your brainstorming and give you something to react to. They should not be viewed as the "correct" answers to the questions.)

- ▶ What kind of stillness is God talking about in this passage? (It's stillness in the midst of chaos. Read the rest of Psalm 46. This verse is talking about far more than having a daily quiet time to pray, though that is certainly something we need. Psalm 46 tells us that in the midst of the unthinkable, "God is our refuge and strength, an ever-present help in trouble" [v. 1].)

- ▶ What situations have arisen in your life where you desperately needed to rest in this stillness, trusting in God as your refuge and strength? (Chaos can come at any time. It shows us how we are utterly out of control of our circumstances. The loss of a job, a divorce, and the death of a loved one are a few examples of situations that often bring chaos.)

- ▶ How can you always rest in stillness, looking to God as your refuge and strength? (The easiest solution is to make prayer and listening to God a daily practice. Set aside time every day to listen expectantly before or after you offer your adoration, confession, thanksgiving, and supplication to God. Like an athlete prepares for a competition, through practicing resting in God's strength you will be better equipped not to allow your focus to be taken away from God when chaos comes.)

Pray together, praising God for His perfections—His infinite and eternal nature, which means that He has no beginning or end; His unchanging nature; His self-sufficiency, which means He has no needs; His omnipotence, which means He's all-powerful; His omniscience, which means He's all-knowing; His omnipresence, which means He's everywhere; His wisdom; His faithfulness; His goodness; His justice; His mercy; His grace; His love; His holiness; and His glory. Ask Him to remind you, through the prompting of His Holy Spirit, to "be still" every day so that you might be reminded on a daily basis that He is God.

Suggested devotion from *The Love Languages Devotional Bible*, page 468 (If We Will Pray)

INDOOR BIKE TOUR

This adventure offers an opportunity to enjoy a scenic route, get a mild workout, and engage in a breezy conversation with your spouse—all from the comfort of your living room. All you need are a pair of indoor bikes or pedaling devices, a travelogue video, and the imagination to pretend that you're cycling somewhere else.

12

GOING THE EXTRA MILE

You can go all-in on the sensory experience of riding a bike through a distant land. You can place space heaters nearby to simulate a warm climate. You can position fans to simulate the effect of a gentle breeze— or a strong headwind. You can prepare water bottles, protein bars, and other essentials in small backpacks. Helmets are optional.

MAKING IT WORK FOR YOU

You have several options for indoor riding, depending on the amount of space you have available. You can use indoor trainer stands for your actual bicycles. You can use upright or recumbent stationary bikes. You can sit in chairs and use under-the-desk pedaling devices. If you don't own the necessary equipment and don't want to buy it, you may be able to borrow it from your cycling-enthusiast friends.

You can find a variety of virtual bike rides online. If you use the search terms "point-of-view bike ride" or "point-of-view cycling" (or some similar combination), you'll find plenty of rides to choose from. Some are nice and leisurely; others are a little more precarious. Choose the ones that best suit your purposes. If you have a video projector, you could screen the footage on a wall to enhance the sensation of actually being there.

For a different and more vigorous riding experience, you could substitute the point-of-view video with movies such as *Breaking Away* and *American Flyers*, which feature cycling races. When the characters onscreen pedal hard, you pedal hard. When they relax, you relax.

SPEAKING THE RIGHT LANGUAGE

Since crashing isn't an issue, and since there are no traffic laws to obey or handlebars to grip, you and your spouse can hold hands while you ride. That's an especially meaningful opportunity if Physical Touch is your spouse's primary love language.

WEAVING THE THIRD STRAND

Read together 1 Timothy 4:8:

"For physical training is of some value, but godliness has value for all things, holding promise for both the present life and the life to come."

Use the following questions as needed to guide your discussion of the passage. (Please note that the responses in parentheses are merely suggestions, ideas to stimulate your brainstorming and give you something to react to. They should not be viewed as the "correct" answers to the questions.)

- ► What is godliness? (It is an intentional effort to pattern your life after Christ—to love the things that He loves, to oppose the things that He opposes, to give priority to the things that are important to Him, and to interact with people in ways that reflect His loving character.)

- ► Why is it so much better than physical training? (Physical training is essential for good health, but its benefits are temporary. The rewards of godliness are eternal.)

- ► Why is godliness valuable in this present life? (It enables us to make God-honoring decisions in every area of our lives. It keeps us aligned with His will.)

- ► Why is it valuable in the life to come? (God's Word suggests that God will reward people—*beyond* giving them eternal life—for their faithful service to Him.)

► How do you train yourself in godliness? (You study Scripture in order to discover what God is like, what He values, and what He expects from His people. You stay in close communication with Him through prayer. You prove yourself faithful in small things so that He entrusts you with bigger things.)

Pray together, thanking God for your health—and for the opportunity to bring glory and honor to Him with the things you do with your body. Ask Him to help you pursue godliness in every area of your life to complement your physical fitness.

Suggested devotion from *The Love Languages Devotional Bible*, page 1121 (Spiritual Growth)

CURATE A COLLECTION

This activity is especially for someone with a collector's mentality. If you or your spouse have a collection—whether it's comic books, stamps, coins, dolls, antiques, records, or something else—spend some time immersed in it together. The idea is that the collector can share his or her passion and the noncollector can share in it.

13

GOING THE EXTRA MILE

If the collection you're curating has potential monetary value, arrange to have it appraised by a professional. You can find reputable appraisers by asking for recommendations from other collectors or by searching online. If the collection is too large or complicated to be appraised as a whole, choose a few of the most valuable pieces for appraisal. If you don't want to go to the trouble or expense of bringing in an appraiser, you can always consult price guides and do your own appraisal.

Even if you have no intention of ever selling your collection, it's helpful to have a ballpark valuation so you know how much to insure it for.

MAKING IT WORK FOR YOU

Depending on the collection, you may choose to organize and clean individual pieces. You may experiment with new ways to store or display the collection. You may catalog information about each piece in an online database for easy reference. You may visit websites devoted to your particular collection in order to gather information. You may ensure that the most valuable pieces are properly  protected. You may work with your spouse to create a wish list that friends and family members can access when they're looking to buy a birthday or Christmas present.

You don't necessarily have to *accomplish* anything. This adventure simply offers the opportunity for a husband or wife to understand his or her collector spouse a little better.

 ## SPEAKING THE RIGHT LANGUAGE

This activity will have special resonance for a collector whose primary love language is Quality Time. You can facilitate that by taking a genuine interest in your spouse's hobby. Ask probing questions. Find out which pieces are most valuable, which ones were the first he or she acquired, and which ones have a sentimental value. Talk about what the collection means to your spouse—what he or she gets from it. Encourage your spouse to "geek out" as you spend quality time together.

WEAVING THE THIRD STRAND

Read 1 Corinthians 10:23 together:

> "'I have the right to do anything,' you say—but not everything is beneficial. 'I have the right to do anything'—but not everything is constructive."

Use the following questions as needed to guide your discussion of the passage. (Please note that the responses in parentheses are merely suggestions, ideas to stimulate your brainstorming and give you something to react to. They should not be viewed as the "correct" answers to the questions.)

- ▶ Why did some Christians in Paul's day claim that they had "the right to do anything"? (They were exercising their Christian liberty, the fact that God gives us freedom to make individual choices in our walk with Christ.)

- ▶ "The right to do anything" that they referred to likely included the way they spent their money and time. What guidelines does God put in those areas? (He wants us to spend our time and money in ways that are beneficial and constructive.)

- ▶ How do you know whether a hobby or pastime is beneficial or constructive? (If it helps you relax or temporarily takes your mind off the pressures and problems of the day, that's great. But when a hobby or pastime is beneficial to your spouse, that is even better.)

► When might a hobby or pastime cross the line and become something that's harmful or destructive? (If it takes away from the time you spend with God or your family—or if it begins to consume too much of your attention or resources—it's counterproductive.)

Pray together, thanking God for the freedom He gives us. Ask Him to guide your decision-making by His Holy Spirit so your freedom does not negatively affect your relationship with Christ and each other.

Suggested devotion from *The Love Languages Devotional Bible*, page 1301 (Empathetic Listening)

A MEAL WITH A NEW FRIEND

Invite an elderly widow or widower—or any elderly person who may be struggling with loneliness or who may enjoy some company—to dinner with you and your spouse, your treat. Get to know one another as you enjoy a meal together. See if you can start a meaningful friendship.

14

GOING THE EXTRA MILE

If your initial outing is a success, take steps to solidify your new acquaintance. This isn't a process to be taken lightly, especially if the person is truly lonely or has no one else to depend on. You will be a godsend and, very likely, an answer to prayer in the person's life—but you need to ensure that you and your spouse are ready for the responsibility that comes with it.

Your best bet is to start slow and gradually work your way into one another's lives. Set a standing date every week to get together. Talk about your lives. Encourage your new friend to open up about his or her needs and struggles. To the extent that you're able, make yourself available to help, whether it involves helping the person do his or her shopping, providing transportation to and from doctor's appointments, or taking care of household chores that have become too difficult for the person.

MAKING IT WORK FOR YOU

Chances are, you know someone from church or from your neighborhood who's widowed and may be looking for companionship—and perhaps some assistance. If not, talk to your pastor or other people in your church or community. Someone will know someone who would be grateful to spend time with you and your spouse.

The plans you make will depend on the person. Be sensitive to his or her needs and concerns. If physical restrictions keep the person from going out, bring a meal to his or her home.

Be prepared with questions to keep the conversation flowing. Here are a few discussion prompts to get you started:

- ► How did you meet your spouse? Was it love at first sight?

- ► What's the secret to a lasting marriage?

- ► Tell me about your family. Do you have any pictures?

- ► How many different cities and states have you lived in? Which one was your favorite? What did you like about each one?

- ► Which teams do you root for?

- ► Tell me about the different jobs you've worked.

- ► What are your hobbies?

If the person seems comfortable talking about a subject, pursue it with some follow-up questions. If not, change the subject or shift the conversation to yourself.

SPEAKING THE RIGHT LANGUAGE

Don't wait for absence to make your heart grow fonder. After spending time with your widowed friend, bask in the opportunity you still have to spend time with your spouse. Take a walk together and say the things that need to be said—about how blessed you are to be able to experience life together, about how your partner has changed you for the better, and about how you can't imagine life without him or her. Such an experience and conversation will likely have an especially profound effect on someone whose primary love language is Quality Time.

WEAVING THE THIRD STRAND

Read together the following passages:

► Psalm 68:5: "A father to the fatherless, a defender of widows, is God in his holy dwelling."

► James 1:27: "Religion that God our Father accepts as pure and faultless is this: to look after orphans and widows in their distress and to keep oneself from being polluted by the world."

Use the following questions as needed to guide your discussion of the passages. (Please note that the responses in parentheses are merely suggestions, ideas to stimulate your brainstorming and give you something to react to. They should not be viewed as the "correct" answers to the questions.)

- ▶ Why, in His Word, does God place such an emphasis on helping widows? (In biblical times, families were expected to take care of their own. A person without a family—especially a *woman* without a family—was extremely vulnerable. She had no one to take care of her, so God stepped into the role.)

- ▶ How does God take care of widows? (There are passages in the Bible in which He miraculously intervenes in the life of a widow. For the most part, however, He leaves that responsibility to His people.)

Pray together, praising God for the fact that no one is overlooked in His field of vision. Ask Him to give you the wisdom, courage, and motivation you need in order to make a difference in the life of someone who needs you.

Suggested devotion from *The Love Languages Devotional Bible*, page 396 (Overflowing)

PHRASES THAT PAY

Once upon a time, a late-night talk show host challenged an NBA star to work three random phrases into a postgame interview. The phrases had nothing to do with basketball and had no context to anything else, really. Still, the player managed to work them into his answers. In the spirit of that accomplishment, here's a modified version of the challenge for you and your spouse to attempt.

15

GOING THE EXTRA MILE

Social media is filled with clips of people saying and doing awkward things. Here's your opportunity to join the throng. While one of you attempts to work a nonsense phrase into a sensible conversation, the other should discreetly record it. If you get interesting reactions from other people in conversations, post the results online—after securing the necessary permission, of course. Your goal is not so much to "go viral" but to have a memento of your adventure.

MAKING IT WORK FOR YOU

Many of the adventures and ideas in this book are designed to bring you and your spouse closer together, to show you a new perspective on your relationship, to make a difference in your lives and in the lives of others. This is not one of those adventures. This idea is pure silliness for the sake of fun and adventure.

To prepare for it, the two of you will need to brainstorm a list of words and phrases that a person wouldn't expect to hear in a normal, everyday conversation—the stranger, the better. Here are a few ideas to get you started:

- ► "rich Corinthian leather"

- ► "crazy as a hypnotized water buffalo"

- ► "troubled glass"

- ► "multicolored belly button lint"

- ► "gravy boat politics"

- ► "2:45 p.m. in the morning"

- ► "faster than a couch"

Some people may laugh at your absurdities. Others may play along. Some may question you. Others may walk away shaking their heads. Whatever response you get, in order for the attempt to count, you may not explain yourself or give any indication whatsoever that you're joking. You have to play it straight.

SPEAKING THE RIGHT LANGUAGE

Surprise your spouse by working compliments and positive statements about him or her into random conversations. You'll want to make sure that your spouse is within earshot, of course—especially if Words of Affirmation is his or her primary love language.

WEAVING THE THIRD STRAND

Talk about how it's okay to occasionally have fun with the things we say. However, when it comes to serious matters, God holds His people to a higher verbal standard.

Read together James 5:12:

> "But let your 'Yes' be 'Yes,' and your 'No,' 'No,' lest you fall into judgment" (NKJV).

Use the following questions as needed to guide your discussion of the passage. (Please note that the responses in parentheses are merely suggestions, ideas to stimulate your brainstorming and give you something to react to. They should not be viewed as the "correct" answers to the questions.)

▶ What does it mean to "let your 'Yes' be 'Yes,' and your 'No,' 'No'"? (It means to be purposeful, straightforward, and honest in the things you say.)

▶ Why is that important, especially for disciples of Jesus? (People need to know that they can trust what we say. They need to know that we value truth and are committed to communicating it in a loving way.)

- Why is it sometimes tempting to add "flourish" to our words? (Verbal flourishes often accompany efforts to mislead or deceive. People who don't want others to focus on the message of their words try to distract by using double-talk or vague and noncommittal words.)

- How can you honor God in the way you talk? (You can practice "speaking the truth in love" [Eph. 4:15]— establishing yourself as someone who can be counted on to speak the truth in a caring way, even if that truth is difficult to hear.)

Pray together, thanking God for giving us communication guidelines that are meant to encourage, motivate, and inspire us. Ask Him to work by His Holy Spirit to guide your tongue so people will look to you for truth, spoken in a loving manner.

Suggested devotion from *The Love Languages Devotional Bible*, page 63
(The Risks of Integrity)

SOUNDTRACK

Spend some time thinking about the arc of your relationship with your spouse—not just the highs and lows, but also the people, places, and things that played a role in it. Look for songs together that correspond with that arc. Create a playlist with your spouse that tells the story of your relationship.

16

GOING THE EXTRA MILE

You have several different options for expanding this idea. The first is to bring out photo albums to remind you of places you've been, things you've done, and experiences you've had. Let the images inspire your song choices.

A second option, if you're so inclined (and gifted), is to *write* a song that celebrates your relationship. You don't necessarily have to compose words and music from scratch. You could simply adapt an existing song by changing the lyrics slightly to make it more personal.

A third option is to post your playlist on a streaming site for others to enjoy and be inspired by.

MAKING IT WORK FOR YOU

Anyone can compile a list of well-known love songs or romantic standards. That's not what this activity is about. This is about finding songs that trace the actual arc of *your* relationship with your spouse—songs that reflect a variety of time periods, locations, events, and moods.

For example, you might begin your playlist with songs that reflect the excitement and confusion of the beginning stages of love. Obviously, you'll want to include songs that have special meaning to you—perhaps the first song you ever danced to or one that you did as a karaoke duet on one of your early dates.

Be sure you paint a complete picture with your playlist. If there were periods of struggle—a bout of jealousy here, a brief breakup there—choose songs that tell those stories. If you moved to a certain area of the country, choose songs that reflect the place and time of your move. If you had children or lost parents or loved ones, choose songs that touch on those milestones.

Your goal is to create a playlist that, if it were stumbled upon by someone who doesn't know you, would do a pretty good job of telling in song the story of your relationship with your spouse.

SPEAKING THE RIGHT LANGUAGE

Surely, some of the songs you choose will make you and your spouse feel like dancing. Don't resist the urge. In fact, if Physical Touch is your spouse's primary love language, make sure you pull him or her close for at least a few steps *every* time a danceable song plays.

WEAVING THE THIRD STRAND

Read together Psalm 150:

"Praise the LORD. Praise God in his sanctuary; praise him in his mighty heavens. Praise him for his acts of power; praise him for his surpassing greatness. Praise him with the sounding of the trumpet, praise him with the harp and lyre, praise him with timbrel and dancing, praise him with the strings and pipe, praise him with the clash of cymbals, praise him with resounding cymbals. Let everything that has breath praise the LORD. Praise the LORD."

Use the following questions as needed to guide your discussion of the passage. (Please note that the responses in parentheses are merely suggestions, ideas to stimulate your brainstorming and give you something to react to. They should not be viewed as the "correct" answers to the questions.)

► Why does music have such a powerful influence on people? (Since music plays such a key role in worship in the Bible, you might say that God created us to be influenced by music—and to influence others with it. In other words, we're wired to react to music.)

► What does music mean to you? (For many people, music amplifies experiences; it makes things memorable. For others, music brings back memories of better times. For others, music expresses emotions that they wouldn't otherwise be able to express.)

► How can you use music to enhance your relationship with God? (Certain types of music can prepare your heart for worship. If you're musically inclined, you might create your own psalms as part of your prayer and quiet time.)

Pray together, thanking God for His gift of music. Ask Him to help you use music and other creative elements to enhance your relationship with Him.

Suggested devotion from *The Love Languages Devotional Bible*, page 584 (Praise Be)

PLAN YOUR DREAM VACATION

You may not be in a financial position to take your dream vacation this year. You may not even be in a financial position to take your dream vacation this *decade*. But why let such details stand in the way of a little anticipation? It's never too early to start preparing for your perfect getaway.

17

GOING THE EXTRA MILE

Once you decide on a destination for your dream getaway, talk to your friends and family members who have vacationed there. Ask them to send you brief video clips of their vacation, including highlights of places that you might want to visit on your own vacation. Watch the clips together to get a sneak preview of your trip. If you don't know anyone who has vacationed where you want to go, do an online search for videos.

MAKING IT WORK FOR YOU

Here's your chance to dream big. If you and your spouse could spend a week—or two weeks—anywhere on earth, where would you choose? What kind of accommodations would you want? How would you travel there? What would you want to do while you're there?

This is more than dreaming, however; this is advance planning. If you decide that you want to stay in a four-star hotel, do an online search for four-star hotels in the area. Explore your options. Do you want a beachside view? A room that opens to the pool? A deluxe suite?

While you're there, would you like to take a dinner cruise? Go parasailing or snorkeling? Visit local museums and points of interest? Fill your itinerary with the things you would really like to do. Remember, this is your *dream* vacation.

As you make your plans, talk about the importance of "counting the cost" before you commit to something as big as a dream vacation—or any major event or opportunity in your life.

SPEAKING THE RIGHT LANGUAGE

If Receiving Gifts is the primary love language of your spouse, you can make this activity memorable by buying a souvenir of your vacation *before* you take it. Order a T-shirt, coffee mug, snow globe, or some other memento of the place you're planning to visit and give it to your spouse as a reminder of what you have to look forward to.

WEAVING THE THIRD STRAND

Read together John 14:1–11. In the passage, Jesus tells His followers that He is returning to His Father's house so He can prepare a place for them to come and dwell with Him. Thomas, one of the disciples, asks a great question:

"Lord, we don't know where you are going, so how can we know the way?" (v. 5). The boldness of Jesus' reply is shocking: "I am the way and the truth and the life. No one comes to the Father except through me." (v. 6).

No matter how much planning you do before a vacation, if you set off thinking you've prepared for every possible circumstance, think again. If your plans are fixed and inflexible, the vacation is going to have more stress and anxiety than joy and relaxation. Just as we have to be mindful that every vacation can have unexpected twists and turns, we have to remember that following Jesus—the only way, the truth, and the life— may not always go as we expect. Just like Thomas, we often want to know ahead of time where Jesus is going and where He is leading us in life, and sometimes we even project our own ambitions and expectations onto Him. We must be careful not to make the mistake of trying to fit Jesus into our own idea of who God is and what He has in store for us but instead trust Him to guide us on the journey with the Holy Spirit. Following Jesus is full of anything but the expected.

Use the following questions as needed to guide your discussion of the passage. (Please note that the responses in parentheses are merely suggestions, ideas to stimulate your brainstorming and give you something to react to. They should not be viewed as the "correct" answers to the questions.)

- ▶ Have you ever been surprised by the unexpected during a vacation? How did you respond to the change in plans? (Perhaps you accepted the change and trusted that things would work out, or perhaps you struggled with the stress of your well-laid plans unraveling.)

- Why does Jesus' claim in verse 6 make people uncomfortable? (It is much more comfortable and accepted in society to believe that all religions bear some kind of witness to the truth.)

- How can we proclaim the message of verse 6 faithfully and humbly? (In John 14, Jesus was teaching His disciples before giving His life on the cross—the ultimate act of love. It is only when we fully trust Jesus and follow His example in loving other people that we can faithfully and humbly make the claim of verse 6.)

Pray together, thanking the Lord for the opportunity to serve as disciples. Ask Him to help you maintain a godly perspective on your service, especially when the cost of service seems high.

Suggested devotion from *The Love Languages Devotional Bible*, page 40 (The Choice to Forgive)

A FAMILIAR PUZZLE

Choose a favorite photo. Send it to a jigsaw puzzle maker. When you get the puzzle back, spread out the pieces on a table and begin working on it together. Don't tell your spouse right away what the puzzle shows. See how long it takes him or her to recognize the picture.

18

GOING THE EXTRA MILE

Make arrangements to re-create the photo in your puzzle. This will be especially challenging (and ultimately rewarding) if there are several people in it. Find the original location where the picture was taken. If that's not possible, look for a convincing substitute location.

Have the people in the photo dress in clothes that are as similar as possible to the clothes in the photo. Recruit a photographer to help get people in the proper positions and take the photo. If you're okay with the idea, post the two photos side by side on social media.

MAKING IT WORK FOR YOU

Choose your photo carefully. It doesn't matter whether it shows just your spouse, just the two of you, or your entire family. What matters is that it works as a jigsaw puzzle. Make sure that the photo you choose has plenty of color contrast and distinguishing features that will come in handy as you try to put pieces together.

You can find a variety of jigsaw puzzle makers online who can create a custom-designed puzzle from your photograph. You'll need to decide how big you want the puzzle to be and how many pieces you want in it. For a relatively quick adventure, choose 250 pieces; for an all-day engagement, choose 1,000.

While you work on the puzzle, take an inventory of the things in your house that have been broken (perhaps into pieces, like the puzzle) and put back together again (or just simply repaired). Change the focus slightly to talk about *relationships* that have been broken and the difficulty of trying to put them back together again.

SPEAKING THE RIGHT LANGUAGE

If Words of Affirmation is the primary love language of your spouse, you can make this activity extra special by focusing on his or her image in the photo. Talk about why the picture means so much to you. What do you see in your spouse when you look at it? What memories does it bring back?

WEAVING THE THIRD STRAND

Read together Jeremiah 17:14:

"GOD, pick up the pieces. Put me back together again. You are my praise!" (MSG).

Use the following questions as needed to guide your discussion of the passage. (Please note that the responses in parentheses are merely suggestions, ideas to stimulate your brainstorming and give you something to react to. They should not be viewed as the "correct" answers to the questions.)

- ► How would you describe the tone of Jeremiah's words in this passage? (Obviously they come from a place of brokenness. But there's also a confidence in his words. He knows God is able to do what he asks.)

- ► What circumstances might cause someone to make such a request of God? (People can be broken by the betrayal of others—a breakup of a marriage or a friendship. They can also be broken by failure or a crisis of confidence. Jeremiah's request may also be the result of having discovered that he can't put himself back together or resolve his plight. Often we turn to God only as a last, desperate measure. Our pride tells us that *we* should be able to fix what is broken inside of us.)

- ► How does God put someone back together again? (He reminds us of who we are—that is, His creation. He reminds us not only of His love for us but also of His healing power. He surrounds us with people who care about us. He restores our confidence by putting us in positions to succeed.)

▶ What would you say to someone who's trying to pick up the pieces of his or her own life? (Nothing is too broken for God to put together again.)

Pray together, praising God for His healing and restoration. Ask Him to bless your efforts to rebuild what's broken in your own life—and to bring hope to others who are trying to rebuild what's broken in their lives. Ask Him to make you an instrument of His healing.

Suggested devotion from *The Love Languages Devotional Bible*, page 468 (If We Will Pray)

NEWS FROM ANOTHER PLACE

If you and your spouse are news junkies, you're probably well aware of the pressing issues and concerns in your area. But what do you know about a city halfway across the country—or halfway around the world? Here's a chance to find out. Spend a leisurely morning reading a local newspaper from a non-local place.

19

GOING THE EXTRA MILE

Get some context for the stories you'll be reading by doing a little research on the city. Dig into its history, both recent and distant. Trace the arc of the hot-button issues that the people of the city are currently facing. Get a sense of the priorities and political leanings of the citizens. You can make yourself a more informed reader of the newspaper by doing some online research beforehand.

If you start to take a special interest in what you read, you may consider extending your interaction with the paper. Many newspapers offer online subscriptions for a reasonable price.

MAKING IT WORK FOR YOU

Your first step is to decide which newspaper you'd like to read. Many libraries subscribe to a variety of newspapers and make them available to their patrons. As mentioned earlier, online subscriptions make many major news-papers available to anyone anywhere.

If you would prefer to take a more creative approach, you could choose a town or region that interests you—perhaps a place you lived when you were younger or a place you've always wanted to visit. Contact the local newspaper and ask to be sent a copy of the paper. Another option is to ask a friend or family member who lives in a distant city to send you a copy of his or her local newspaper.

Immerse yourselves in the newspaper. If possible, pull up a detailed online map of the region so that you have a sense of its geography and so that you can place the locations of the various stories. Try to get a sense of what the people are like and what's important to them.

Talk about the differences you notice between that area and your hometown. Based on what you read, talk about whether you think you would enjoy living in that area. If you come across stories of loss or devastation, take time to pray for the people involved.

SPEAKING THE RIGHT LANGUAGE

If Acts of Service is the primary love language of your spouse, you have an opportunity to do something memorable as part of this adventure. Prepare your spouse's favorite breakfast foods, along with a cup of coffee or orange juice. Put it all on a tray, along with the not-so-local newspaper, and serve your spouse breakfast in bed.

WEAVING THE THIRD STRAND

Read together the parable of the good Samaritan in Luke 10:25–37. In the parable, people who were "expected" to show concern and care were too busy with their own concerns to tend to someone in need. It was left to the least likely source to offer loving assistance.

Use the following questions as needed to guide your discussion of the passage. (Please note that the responses in parentheses are merely suggestions, ideas to stimulate your brainstorming and give you something to react to. They should not be viewed as the "correct" answers to the questions.)

- ▶ Why did the man ask Jesus who his neighbor was? (He wanted a manageable responsibility, a finite number of people that he had to care about.)

- ▶ According to Jesus' parable, who is our neighbor? (Anyone in need is our neighbor.)

- ▶ What should we take away from the fact that the one who ultimately reached out to the man in need was someone from another land—someone who had no obvious reason to care about him—and someone who was considered inferior? (Our ability—and responsibility—to show loving concern to others has no borders.)

► How can we empathize with people we have no contact with? (We can recognize that they are likely very much like us. Most people share the same basic needs and concerns.)

Pray together, thanking God for giving you so many "neighbors" who care about you. Ask Him to make Himself known in the lives of the people you read about in the newspaper who are struggling or in need. Ask Him to use you to make a difference in other people's lives.

Suggested devotion from *The Love Languages Devotional Bible*, page 338
(Be Kind)

PEOPLE WATCHING—WITH A TWIST

People watching doesn't have to be a passive activity—not if you have a perceptive gaze, a nimble imagination, and a partner willing to engage in some conjecturing about the people you see. Practice your empathy skills by imagining what might be going on in other people's lives.

20

GOING THE EXTRA MILE

You can take this activity to the next level by praying for the people you observe. Try to anticipate their needs by scrutinizing their demeanor. Does one person seem lonely? Does another seem anxious or depressed? Is there a single parent who seems overwhelmed? Is there a couple who seems not to be getting along? Lift them up to God in prayer. Ask Him to work in their lives, to make Himself known, to bring healing and comfort.

Beyond that, you and your spouse could make yourselves instruments of God's comfort. If you see someone in need of immediate help, step in. Introduce your-selves and ask if there's anything you can do to help.

MAKING IT WORK FOR YOU

Find a comfortable place where you and your spouse can sit for a while and watch people pass by. A bench near a walking trail or playground, a table at an outdoor café on a busy street, and a waiting area in an airport terminal would all be ideal locations. You're looking for a vantage point where you can unobtrusively observe a wide variety of people.

Your goal is to look beyond people's appearances. Study their facial expressions, their body language, their interactions with others, and any other clues you can find. Try to get a read on people.

When you see someone who looks especially interesting, imagine a "backstory" for the person. Try to imagine where they

 might be coming from, where they might be going, who they are, what they might be doing, what they might have done in the past, and anything else you can think of. Feel free to romanticize or embellish your stories, according to your imaginative whims. (If that means the elderly woman feeding pigeons is really a dangerous CIA operative, so be it.)

The goal of the exercise is to notice people and to think a little more carefully about their lives.

SPEAKING THE RIGHT LANGUAGE

If your spouse's primary love language is Physical Touch, make a point of holding hands, caressing each other's shoulders, walking with your arms around each other, and engaging in any other kind of PDA you're both comfortable with. Imagine that a couple is watching you in the same way that you're watching others. Talk about what conclusions that couple might draw about your relationship.

WEAVING THE THIRD STRAND

Read Luke 8:43–48. In the passage, a woman who had been suffering from a blood condition for years saw an opportunity to be cured when Jesus passed by. In the midst of a crowd, she quietly touched the hem of Jesus' garment and was immediately healed. Jesus realized what had happened and turned around. "Who touched me?" He asked.

His disciples were confused by His question. *How could He notice one particular person in such a crowd?* they wondered.

Use the following questions as needed to guide your discussion of the passage from there. (Please note that the responses in parentheses are merely suggestions, ideas to stimulate your brainstorming and give you something to react to. They should not be viewed as the "correct" answers to the questions.)

► How was Jesus able to sense what the woman had done? (Aside from the fact that He has supernatural power, He is attuned to the needs of individuals. He recognized what the woman had done because He felt her need. He empathized with her.)

- ► Why were the disciples confused by Jesus' question? (They saw only the crowd—the "big picture." They weren't paying attention to the individuals, the people with very real needs.)

- ► What keeps us from recognizing people's struggles and needs? (We get too focused on our own needs. We make snap judgments and allow preconceived notions to guide the way we think about others.)

Pray together, thanking the Lord for His compassion and healing power. Ask Him to bless your efforts to empathize with others and to recognize their needs and struggles.

Suggested devotion from *The Love Languages Devotional Bible*, page 1092 (Love in the Interruptions)

LEAVE YOUR MARK

Blessed are those who hunger and thirst for righteousness, for they will be filled. Matthew 5:6

21

In Deuteronomy 6:9, Moses instructs the people of Israel to write God's commandments on the doorframes of their houses and on their gates. Here's an opportunity to do something similar in your own home by writing Scripture passages in places that aren't so obvious.

GOING THE EXTRA MILE

Most of the writing you do in this adventure will be small and inconspicuous—detail work that will be obvious only to sharp-eyed observers and people who know where to look for it. But if you're going the extra mile, you might as well go big.

Hire a professional painter or calligrapher to paint one of your favorite Bible passages on a wall in your home. One obvious location would be the wall opposite your front door, so that the verse is the first thing visitors see when they enter your house. Make sure that the verse you choose reflects your family's priorities and sets the right tone—something like, "As for me and my house-hold, we will serve the LORD" (Josh. 24:15).

MAKING IT WORK FOR YOU

All you really need for this adventure are a few fine-point permanent markers and a Bible. Choose your favorite passages of comfort, hope, protection, and promise to write in various places of your home—none of which necessarily have to be visible. Think of them as perpetual words of prayer and thanksgiving, always present throughout your home.

You can have some fun matching Scripture passages and biblical promises to various locations throughout your home. Here are some ideas:

> ► On the inside of a light switch wall plate, you might write, "The light shines in the darkness, and the darkness has not overcome it" (John 1:5).

> ► On the underside of a birdhouse, you might write, "Look at the birds of the air; . . . your heavenly Father feeds them" (Matt. 6:26).

> ► On the underside of your child's bed or crib, you might write, "When you lie down, you will not be afraid; when you lie down, your sleep will be sweet" (Prov. 3:24).

You could really have fun with this adventure if you're planning a remodeling or renovation project in your house. You could write a passage on every exposed two-by-four, if you wanted to.

SPEAKING THE RIGHT LANGUAGE

You can make this adventure especially mean-ingful if Words of Affirmation is your spouse's primary love language. Look for opportunities to write actual words of affirmation in places around your house. For example, on the bottom of a drawer you might write, "He who finds a wife finds what is good and receives favor from the LORD" (Prov. 18:22).

WEAVING THE THIRD STRAND

Read together Deuteronomy 11:18–20:

"Fix these words of mine in your hearts and minds; tie them as symbols on your hands and bind them on your foreheads. Teach them to your children, talking about them when you sit at home and when you walk along the road, when you lie down and when you get up. Write them on the doorframes of your houses and on your gates."

Use the following questions as needed to guide your discussion of the passage. (Please note that the responses in parentheses are merely suggestions, ideas to stimulate your brainstorming and give you something to react to. They should not be viewed as the "correct" answers to the questions.)

▶ What happens when something is constantly set before our eyes? (Advertisers understand the importance of repetitive views. The more we see something, the deeper it imprints itself on our memory.)

- ► Why is it important to commit God's Word—and especially His promises—to memory? (Being able to immediately recall God's Word can help us resist temptation—and can give us courage, comfort, and inspiration when we need them most.)

- ► In addition to writing passages around your house, what are some other ways you and your family can commit God's Word to memory? (You can practice reciting passages together when you're riding in the car. You can quote passages as part of your mealtime and bedtime prayers. You can offer incentives to your kids for memorizing Scripture.)

Pray together, praising God for the power of His Word. Thank Him for the words of promise, hope, encouragement, and inspiration that are found throughout Scripture. Ask Him to help you claim those promises when you're struggling.

Suggested devotion from *The Love Languages Devotional Bible*, page 206 (Story Time)

BUILD A SNOWMAN TO REMEMBER

Do you want to build a snowman? If so, do it in a way that's never been done before. Build a snowman that people will remember long after the snow has melted. Build a snowman that makes people stop and wonder where you came up with such an idea or how you managed to pull it off.

22

GOING THE EXTRA MILE

TV news crews are always on the lookout for unusual local-interest stories—even perhaps the building of an extraordinary snowman. If you create something truly memorable, take a picture of it and post it on the social media sites of your local news stations. If it's a slow news day, one of them may send a camera crew to get footage of your creation. Who knows? Your snowman may get five seconds of airtime and a brief shout-out during a weather segment.

MAKING IT WORK FOR YOU

You could build an upside-down snowman. Put a hat on the bottom and shoes on the top. Wrap a scarf around his "neck" and let it hang down over his face. Use tree branches for arms, which should be extended downward, capped by two mittens that lie palms-flat on the ground. The idea is that the snowman is doing a headstand.

If you have advanced engineering or design skills, you could build a snowman that leans at a precipitous angle. You could create one with two heads.

What you lack in artistic and engineering skills, you could make up for in sheer mass and size. Import snow from other places, if you have to. Create a snowman seven feet tall or more. Make him hugely rotund. Build the Goliath of snowmen.

Reward yourselves for a job well done with mugs of hot cocoa. While you enjoy your warming beverage, talk about how standing out from the crowd—as your snowman does—can be challenging for people. Talk about the different people you know who seem to stand out from the crowd—and what it is that makes them unique.

 ## SPEAKING THE RIGHT LANGUAGE

The underlying biblical principle for this adventure is Psalm 139:14, in which the psalmist acknowledges that he is "fearfully and wonderfully made." In that spirit, while you build your snowman, spend some time talking about specific ways in which your spouse is fearfully and wonderfully made. Focus not just on his or her obvious physical attributes but on intangibles as well—

aspects of his or her character that you admire. If Words of Affirmation is your spouse's primary love language, your heartfelt praise will likely have a big impact.

WEAVING THE THIRD STRAND

Read together Psalm 139:14:

"I praise you because I am fearfully and wonderfully made; your works are wonderful, I know that full well."

Use the following questions as needed to guide your discussion of the passage. (Please note that the responses in parentheses are merely suggestions, ideas to stimulate your brainstorming and give you something to react to. They should not be viewed as the "correct" answers to the questions.)

▶ What does it mean to be fearfully and wonderfully made? (Each person is an extraordinary creation. We share qualities that bind us together, yet we possess individual qualities that set us apart and allow us to make unique contributions to the world.)

▶ Why is it important to acknowledge that we are fearfully and wonderfully made? (Acknowledging the extraordinary nature of our design connects us to our Creator. It offers an unlimited opportunity to praise Him.)

▶ Why is it easy to forget how fearfully and wonderfully made we are? (The media creates and promotes impossible standards of beauty. When we compare ourselves to air-brushed supermodels, we'll always come up short. Also, the world is filled with people who need to put others down in order to feel good about themselves.)

▶ How can we maintain a "Psalm 139:14 attitude" when there are so many forces aligned to make us doubt ourselves? (We can surround ourselves with people who see the good in us. We can question the images of beauty we see in the media. We can ask God to help us see ourselves as He sees us. We can look for the good in others.)

Pray together, thanking God for your fearful and wonderful creation. Ask Him to give you the wisdom to recognize the fearfully wondrous design of others and the courage and kind-heartedness to express it.

Suggested devotion from *The Love Languages Devotional Bible*, page 1329 (Human Worth)

GIVE IT A CHANCE

Everyone has different tastes—in food, books, movies, pastimes. The fact that two people don't share the same tastes doesn't make them incompatible; it makes them individuals. It's inevitable that there are things your spouse likes that you don't—and vice versa. Here's an opportunity to change each other's minds (or not). Each of you will choose one thing for the other to try.

23

GOING THE EXTRA MILE

It would be a shame if you and your spouse tried something new and the result wasn't saved for posterity. Be sure that you get photos or video to document the occasion. You don't have to show anyone, but it would be a nice souvenir to remind you of this adventurous occasion.

Another option is to extend the adventure over an entire weekend, split into two parts. On the first day, one of you will get to set the agenda, planning things for the other to try. On the second day, the other person will do the planning.

MAKING IT WORK FOR YOU

Keep in mind that your ultimate goal is relaxation and enjoyment. For that reason, you want to make sure that whatever you ask your spouse to try doesn't take your spouse too far out of his or her comfort zone. Trying sushi is one thing; jumping out of a plane is something else entirely.

One way to approach this adventure is for each of you to prepare a list of four or five things your spouse hasn't done, and let him or her choose which one to try. The lists may include anything from playing a round of golf to getting a manicure or pedicure to attending a yoga class to going fishing.

Before each of you tries something new, share your feelings about it—your preconceived notions about what it's like. After you've done it, talk about the experience. Did you enjoy it? Did it confirm or defy your preconceived notions? Is it something you would try again? Did it open your mind or cause you to rethink your attitude toward other things?

Be honest and considerate in your responses. If your preconceived notions turned out to be wrong, own up to  it. If, on the other hand, your preconceived notions turned out to be right, don't gloat or say, "I told you so." Remember, whatever it is you did is something your spouse finds enjoyable. To belittle it is to belittle your spouse.

SPEAKING THE RIGHT LANGUAGE

If your spouse's primary love language is Quality Time, you can do something meaningful for him or her just by approaching the adventure with the right attitude. Show excitement, curiosity, and interest in what you're about to do—for the simple reason that your spouse enjoys it.

WEAVING THE THIRD STRAND

Read together Joshua 1:9:

"Have I not commanded you? Be strong and courageous. Do not be afraid; do not be discouraged, for the LORD your God will be with you wherever you go."

Use the following questions as needed to guide your discussion of the passage. (Please note that the responses in parentheses are merely suggestions, ideas to stimulate your brainstorming and give you something to react to. They should not be viewed as the "correct" answers to the questions.)

▶ In this passage, God is speaking to Joshua, who had just become the leader of the Hebrew people after the death of Moses. It was Joshua's responsibility to do what Moses couldn't do: lead the people into the promised land and drive out the nations that had settled there. Considering the circumstances, what fears might Joshua have been wrestling with? (He was replacing one of the greatest leaders who ever lived. The people he was leading were unpredictable. The enemies they were going to face were powerful and intimidating.)

► Why were those fears ultimately irrelevant? (God promised to accompany Joshua and the Hebrew people every step of the way.)

► Why is it important to note that God didn't promise to help Joshua and the Hebrew people avoid the dangers that lay ahead? (God *wants* us to face difficult situations and circumstances that frighten us. That's how we learn to trust Him—by leaning on Him when we lack courage or strength.)

Pray together, thanking God not just for His protection but also for putting you in situations that stretch your faith and bring you closer to Him. Ask Him to give you the wisdom and clarity of mind to recognize His presence in every situation you face.

Suggested devotion from *The Love Languages Devotional Bible*, page 235 (True Prosperity)

DO A MICRO-DECLUTTER

24

Scaling back—simplifying your life by minimizing clutter—is always a good practice. You and your spouse can purge unwanted possessions by targeting one specific area of your house for a thorough going-over.

GOING THE EXTRA MILE

For maximum benefit, you can approach your decluttering adventure as the prelude to a garage sale. As you identify the things you want to get rid of, price them to sell and mark them accordingly. If you plan to divide your proceeds among your family members, you can use different colors of price tags to help you identify which items belong to each person.

Another option is to earmark the proceeds from your garage sale for a specific purpose, whether it's to fund a family vacation, a school trip, or a missions program at church.

MAKING IT WORK FOR YOU

Identify a specific area of your house that you want to declutter. Depending on your time and level of ambition, it may be a room, a closet, or a section of your unfinished basement. Once you've identified the area, get to work. Make sure that you have plenty of boxes and bags on hand so you can sort and haul things away with ease.

You can find any number of principles and strategies for decluttering online or in the self-help section of your local library or bookstore. If one of them resonates with you, follow it.

For the sake of this exercise, however, be sure that you establish one unbreakable rule. Whatever part of your house you choose to declutter, make sure you complete the job. If you set aside a stack of papers to be filed, file them. If you sort out things to be taken to Goodwill, load the car and make the trip. Don't leave any portion of the job for another day. A successful small-scale decluttering project may give you the confidence and momentum you need to tackle something larger in the future.

SPEAKING THE RIGHT LANGUAGE

Some people have difficulty parting with possessions. If your spouse falls into that category, be sensitive. Talk about it. Try to understand his or her feelings. Be willing to compromise if the two of you disagree over whether something should be discarded. If your spouse's primary love language happens to be Quality Time, the time you spend talking through his or her feelings will resonate powerfully as love.

WEAVING THE THIRD STRAND

Read together 1 Corinthians 14:33:

"For God is not a God of disorder but of peace—
as in all the congregations of the Lord's people."

Use the following questions as needed to guide your discussion of the passage. (Please note that the responses in parentheses are merely suggestions, ideas to stimulate your brainstorming and give you something to react to. They should not be viewed as the "correct" answers to the questions.)

- In 1 Corinthians 14, the apostle Paul is talking about maintaining order in worship. Look at verses 26–40. What are some of the things that can cause disorder? (Certain spiritual gifts, such as speaking in tongues, are meant to be used in conjunction with other spiritual gifts, such as the interpretation of tongues. Without the corresponding gift, a worship service can become chaotic.)

- Where else do you see evidence of God's orderliness? (The intricacy of creation and the interconnectedness of life on this planet are evidence of God's sense of order.)

- What are some areas in which disorder can cause problems? (Relationships can be damaged by disorder. People who thrive on chaos in their relationships cause turmoil for everyone around them. A disorderly approach to your work can also wreak havoc on your career.)

▶ How do you maintain order, even when chaos is going on all around you? (You can't do it unless you make it a constant priority. Busyness, obligations, and distractions such as social media and electronic devices threaten to overwhelm our relationships and throw them into chaos. Unless you make time to be together with the people you love—free of distractions and obligations—chaos will always be a threat.)

Pray together, praising God for the astonishing order He established in His creation. Ask Him to give you a heart for order in all your relationships.

Suggested devotion from *The Love Languages Devotional Bible*, page 1310 (Equal Partners)

I WISH

Most wish lists are made up of material things—clothes, toys, tools—especially when it comes to Christmas or birthday lists. Here's a chance to buck the trend. You and your spouse will create and exchange wish lists of nonmaterial items—things you would like to do or have done for you.

25

GOING THE EXTRA MILE

Chances are you have a pretty good idea of at least one or two things that your spouse is likely to wish for. Most of us drop hints about our wish lists in our daily lives without even realizing it. We say things such as "I wish I had time to catch up with my sister" or "I would love to get that basement cleaned out" or "I would really like to get to the pool [or golf course or farmers market or drive-in] one last time before the season ends."

Each one of those things is a potential wish list item. If you pay attention to the verbal and nonverbal clues your spouse offers, you may be able to anticipate something on his or her wish list. Then, before the adventure even begins, you can work to fulfill the wish. And you can amaze your spouse with your predictive powers.

MAKING IT WORK FOR YOU

You don't need a lot of preparation or materials for this adventure—at least, not for this part of it. All you need are two sheets of paper and two pencils. With your supplies in hand, spend some time together creating your individual lists.

Your lists will depend on your unique circumstances. Here are some ideas to get you thinking:

- ► "I wish we could take a new family portrait."

- ► "I wish we could christen our new grill with a cookout for the whole family."

- ► "I wish I could spend all day Saturday in the garden."

- ► "I wish I could visit my father before he has surgery."

- ► "I wish I had time to train for a half marathon."

Once you've compiled your lists, share them with each other. Talk about why each item is meaningful and how long you've been wishing for it. After this initial adventure is over, the real adventure begins. Make plans to fulfill as many items as possible on each other's lists.

SPEAKING THE RIGHT LANGUAGE

If Physical Touch is your spouse's primary love language, you can make this adventure memorable by including a touch-intensive item on your wish list. For example, you might write, "I want to learn how to give you an ultra-relaxing massage." From there, you can plan a "training session," in which you try different massage techniques on your spouse.

WEAVING THE THIRD STRAND

Read together the following passages:

▶ John 15:7: "If you remain in me and my words remain in you, ask whatever you wish, and it will be done for you."

▶ Matthew 7:7: "Ask and it will be given to you; seek and you will find; knock and the door will be opened to you."

Use the following questions as needed to guide your discussion of the passages. (Please note that the responses in parentheses are merely suggestions, ideas to stimulate your brainstorming and give you something to react to. They should not be viewed as the "correct" answers to the questions.)

▶ What does it mean to "remain" in the Lord and have His words remain in us? (It means to make His will our top priority.)

▶ What keeps us from asking, seeking, and knocking in our prayer time? (In some cases, we may underestimate

God's desire to bless us. In others cases, the distractions and obstacles that life throws at us every day may keep us from maximizing our prayer time.)

▶ How do you determine what you pray for and what you take care of yourself? (Sometimes in prayer, we opt not to bother God with the "small stuff." If something seems simple or within our power, we may be inclined to tackle it ourselves. When we do that, however, we miss out on an opportunity to involve God in every area of our lives.)

▶ How do we keep our prayers from becoming wish lists? (One strategy is to save our requests for the end of our prayers—after we express our praise and adoration, confess our sins, and offer thanksgiving for God's goodness.)

Pray together, thanking God for His open invitation for us to bring our requests, desires, and concerns to Him in prayer. Ask Him to give you the wisdom and guidance you need to maximize your prayer time.

Suggested devotion from *The Love Languages Devotional Bible*, page 306 (Intercession)

MEMES FOR YOU

Memes—images, texts, or brief video clips that deliver messages—have become wildly popular on social media. Embrace the trend for a quick and fun adventure in which you and your spouse exchange memes that have meaning and purpose to you.

26

GOING THE EXTRA MILE

You can find a variety of meme generator sites online. Most offer the option of adding captions to existing photos or illustrations or uploading and captioning your own. Choose the option that works best for you to create an original meme especially for your spouse.

You don't have to share the meme with anyone, if the two of you would prefer to keep it private. You can save it for your personal correspondence, if you want. Your goal is simply to create something that expresses how you feel about each other.

MAKING IT WORK FOR YOU

To add an element of challenge to this adventure, set a time limit. Give yourselves thirty minutes to find three memes that describe your spouse or reflect his or her views—and then to find three memes that describe you or reflect your views. The memes may be funny or serious, political, parental, or personal—as long as they hit home and aren't offensive or derogatory.

When time is up, share your memes. It will be interesting to see if you touch on similar themes for each other or for yourselves. Talk about what the memes communicate about you. Talk also about what the memes *don't* communicate about you. What aspects of your character and personality would get lost if someone based their opinion of you solely on your memes?

If you'd like to go more in-depth in your discussion, talk about what happens when you use memes. On one hand, you can make someone laugh or acknowledge a personal foible that others can relate to. But is there a downside to using shortcuts like memes and Twitter feeds to communicate? Can it become a stumbling block to more sincere and meaningful conversation?

SPEAKING THE RIGHT LANGUAGE

They say a picture is worth a thousand words. If a meme counts as a picture, you can offer your spouse thousands of Words of Affirmation with just a few lovingly chosen memes. If you can't find memes that say exactly what you want, create your own. Post your memes privately or publicly, depending on what your spouse would be most comfortable with.

WEAVING THE THIRD STRAND

Read together Proverbs 26:18–19:

"Like a maniac shooting flaming arrows of death
is one who deceives their neighbor and says, 'I was only joking!'"

Use the following questions as needed to guide your discussion of the passage. (Please note that the responses in parentheses are merely suggestions, ideas to stimulate your brainstorming and give you something to react to. They should not be viewed as the "correct" answers to the questions.)

► Why do you think the author compares deceptive speech such as sarcasm to "a maniac shooting flaming arrows of death"? (Deceptive speech often leaves destruction and misery in its wake. Being laughed at or having your beliefs or feelings minimized through humor can be a painful experience.)

► What's wrong with saying, "I was only joking"? (Not everyone shares the same sense of humor. Something that is a joke to one person may seem very real to another. There's wisdom in the old saying "Many a true word is spoken in jest." To say "I was only joking" is to ignore the pain that ill-conceived jokes can cause.)

- ► Why do you think sarcasm is so prevalent in social media? (The anonymous and impersonal nature of social media gives people courage to say things that they might not say in a face-to-face setting. Sincerity is often mocked in social media.)

Pray together, thanking God for the opportunity to have your voice be heard in the broad context of social media. Ask Him to work through His Holy Spirit to guide your words so that they are uplifting and provide encouragement and communicate His wisdom and truth to others.

Suggested devotion from *The Love Languages Devotional Bible*, page 697
(Someone's Ears Are Burning)

LIFESAVERS

Do you have the training to assist someone in an emergency until medical personnel arrive? Would you know what to do if someone stopped breathing? Here's an opportunity for you and your spouse to learn vital skills together—skills that may one day prove to be a matter of life and death.

27

GOING THE EXTRA MILE

There is no downside to going the extra mile in this case. With a certain amount of training, you both can become certified in CPR and first aid. You can qualify as instructors. You can teach your kids, your extended family, and your friends and neighbors how to become lifesavers. You can lead an effort in your workplaces to provide training to employees. From this single adventure, you can create a mini army of potential lifesavers, people qualified to step in and make a difference in the event of an emergency. Imagine the number of lives that could be influenced.

MAKING IT WORK FOR YOU

The best place to start this adventure is with your local Red Cross. There you will find several different options—including online classes. One of the most popular courses teaches CPR, the resuscitation technique that has saved countless lives.

Another option is to take a first-aid class, which trains laypeople how to provide assistance in times of crisis. In this course, you and your spouse will learn the latest techniques for administering first aid to someone suffering from an asthma-related emergency, anaphylactic shock, a diabetic emergency, a heart attack, a stroke, or an epileptic seizure. You'll learn the best strategies for helping a choking victim, someone who's suffered a severe burn or cut, or someone who has ingested poison.

One of the great things about taking a class together is that you have someone to review the lessons with—and, more significantly, someone to practice with. (That prospect will be especially appealing if Physical Touch is your spouse's or your primary love language.)

What could be more satisfying—and potentially beneficial—than equipping yourselves together to make a profound difference in other people's lives?

SPEAKING THE RIGHT LANGUAGE

If Receiving Gifts is the primary love language of your spouse, you can put a profound exclamation point on this adventure with one simple, inexpensive present. Buy a roll of Life Savers candy or mints for each of you—not to be eaten, but to be carried around in your pocket, purse, or car glove compartment as a reminder of your training and your potential in the event of an emergency.

WEAVING THE THIRD STRAND

Read together Luke 9:1–6, the account of Jesus sending His disciples to minister and heal:

> "When Jesus had called the Twelve together, he gave them power and authority to drive out all demons and to cure diseases" (v. 1).

Use the following questions as needed to guide your discussion of the passage. (Please note that the responses in parentheses are merely suggestions, ideas to stimulate your brainstorming and give you something to react to. They should not be viewed as the "correct" answers to the questions.)

- ▶ What did Jesus' equipping of His disciples include? (He gave them the power to drive out demons, cure diseases, proclaim the kingdom of God, and heal the sick.)

- ▶ How would the disciples know how to drive out demons, cure diseases, and heal sickness? (Mark 9:14–29 offers a glimpse of the disciples' training. In the passage, some of the disciples fail to exorcise a demon from a young boy. When Jesus learns of their failure, He drives out the demon. Afterward, the disciples go to Jesus privately and ask what they did wrong. "This kind can come out only by prayer," He explains (v. 29). The passage suggests that the disciples were able to pick Jesus' brain. Not only were they able to observe Him day in and day out, but they received specialized training in the specifics of ministry.)

► Why do you think Jesus' instructions to His disciples included physical ministry as well as spiritual ministry? (The physical ministry opened people's hearts and minds to the spiritual ministry. Jesus demonstrated that He cared about every part of people's well-being.)

► Why is a hands-on ministry so powerful? (Nothing communicates love more powerfully than working to meet someone's most pressing needs. "Getting your hands dirty" to help someone in need says more about the Lord you serve than any words ever could.)

Pray together, thanking God for saving your eternal life. Ask Him to make you an instrument of His healing—to help you be prepared to intervene when people are in need.

Suggested devotion from *The Love Languages Devotional Bible*, page 210 (Serving Together)

BEAT THE CLOCK

How quickly can you clean the kitchen after a big meal? How fast can you detail the interior and exterior of your car? How long would it take you to empty every wastebasket in your house if you were working at top speed? You can answer those questions and others with this adventure. Working with—and occasionally competing with—your spouse, your quest is to see how fast you can accomplish household tasks.

28

GOING THE EXTRA MILE

If you want to put some extra effort into this adventure, you could establish a baseline for various tasks. You'll need to do a little research to get an estimate of how long certain jobs usually take. The next time you clean the living room, wash the dishes, empty the wastebaskets, scrub toilets, clear the gutters, or dust the furniture, time yourself. See how long it takes you to complete the task, working at a leisurely pace. Keep track of these baseline times in a notebook or on your personal device. Let them serve as times to beat for your adventure.

MAKING IT WORK FOR YOU

Some adventures can be planned as specific events; others can be created on the spur of the moment to make routine events or dull situations more exciting. This adventure falls into the latter category. The routine events in question are your weekly chores—the necessary household tasks that can swallow an entire Saturday. You can't avoid the chores—at least, not without consequences—but you can make them more interesting by tapping into your competitive nature.

All you need is a stopwatch and a list of things to be done. Time yourselves to see how quickly you can finish each assignment. Afterward, you can compare results as you celebrate with some pizza or ice cream.

Needless to say, finishing a chore quickly does no good if the job isn't done well. So you'll need to maintain certain standards of quality as well. If you and your spouse work separately, you might set a rule that one person's work has to pass the inspection of the other in order for it to count. If you want to carry the adventure to its logical extreme, you could assign fifteen-, thirty-, or sixty-second penalties for jobs that are incomplete.

If you jot down your times for each task, you can create a family "record book." Next to each household chore, write down the record time in which that chore was accomplished. Keep the record book in a place where everyone can see it. Let it serve as motivation to the rest of your family members as they do household chores.

SPEAKING THE RIGHT LANGUAGE

If Quality Time is your spouse's primary love language, you can make chore day extra special by working as a team. You can have a lot of fun together as you try to figure out the most efficient ways to work with and around each other to accomplish each task.

WEAVING THE THIRD STRAND

Read together Colossians 3:23–24:

"Whatever you do, work at it with all your heart, as working for the Lord, not for human masters, since you know that you will receive an inheritance from the Lord as a reward. It is the Lord Christ you are serving."

Use the following questions as needed to guide your discussion of the passage. (Please note that the responses in parentheses are merely suggestions, ideas to stimulate your brainstorming and give you something to react to. They should not be viewed as the "correct" answers to the questions.)

► What's the difference between working for human masters and working for God? (Human masters often treat people dishonestly. They try to take advantage of them. They may not always recognize people's potential. God, on the other hand, knows everything about our potential because He gave it to us.)

► How do you work for the Lord with all your heart? (You put your God-given gifts to use. You give the kind of effort you would want someone to give you. You look for opportunities to help others. You give Him the glory.)

► What happens when other people see a God-honoring work ethic in you? (For one thing, you gain respect. Most people respect someone who's willing to work hard. More importantly, however, you focus people's attention on the Lord you serve—the One who gave you the skills and abilities to work.)

Pray together, thanking God for the opportunity we have to work for Him—and for the inheritance that awaits us. Ask Him to help you maintain your focus on His work and avoid being distracted by less important things.

Suggested devotion from *The Love Languages Devotional Bible*, page 105 (The Ethics of Work)

SAVE IT FOR A RAINY DAY

Rain has gotten a bad rap as a killjoy—the reason that baseball games, picnics, and other fun activities are canceled. Here's your chance to change some perceptions. Instead of allowing rain to cancel your plans, make plans that will be enhanced by falling precipitation.

29

GOING THE EXTRA MILE

Make your own video to the classic song "Singin' in the Rain." During a downpour, visit a number of interesting locations in your area. At each spot, record yourselves lip-syncing a portion of the song while the rain falls around you. If you can locate a pair of umbrellas, a pair of fedoras, and a lamppost, you might even re-create a portion of Gene Kelly's famous dance from the movie of the same name. Edit your clips together and post the video for your friends and family members to enjoy on social media.

MAKING IT WORK FOR YOU

What you choose to do during your rainy-day activity will depend on your location and your interests. If you live near water, plan a leisurely stroll on the beach during a downpour. Better yet, play in the water. As long as there's no lightning, why not?

If you're landlocked, plan a hike through a local forest preserve or state park. Deep in the woods, you can enjoy some natural shelter—not to mention the really cool sound of rain pelting the leaves.

If you're feeling sporty, play a tennis match in the rain. Challenge your spouse to a game of one-on-one basketball. Go for a long run. See if you can slide down a hill on the wet grass. If you have a dog that might like to frolic in the rain, include him or her in your adventure. Whatever you do, just be sure you stay safe.

SPEAKING THE RIGHT LANGUAGE

If your spouse's primary love language is Quality Time, you can make this adventure especially meaningful by spending a portion of your day taking pictures together. Wherever you go and whatever you do on your rainy day, capture it in digital form. Before you do, however, spend some quality time setting up and posing for each shot.

WEAVING THE THIRD STRAND

Read Psalm 72:1–7 together. In the passage, Solomon, the new king of Israel, asks the Lord to bless his reign so the people of his kingdom will prosper. Referring to himself in verse 6, Solomon prays, "May he be like rain falling on a mown field, like showers watering the earth."

Use the following questions as needed to guide your discussion of the passage. (Please note that the responses in parentheses are merely suggestions, ideas to stimulate your brainstorming and give you something to react to. They should not be viewed as the "correct" answers to the questions.)

- ▶ Why did Solomon use the image of rain falling on a mown field? (Rain not only refreshes the ground but also spurs growth. Solomon wanted to help Israel flourish and reach its full growth potential.)

- ▶ How did God respond to Solomon's request? (He blessed Solomon beyond measure—not just in wisdom, but in riches and power as well. Under Solomon, Israel reached the height of its power, influence, wealth, and security.)

- ▶ What can we learn about prayer from Solomon's words in Psalm 72? (Solomon asked God to equip him so that he could serve the Lord in a powerful way and make a difference in other people's lives. That's the kind of prayer that pleases God.)

- ▶ Solomon was facing a situation that few people ever faced. He had been chosen to serve as king of Israel. Why do his words in Psalm 72 still have such powerful meaning for non-royals? (Most people would like to have that kind of impact on others. Parents especially would love to influence their children in the way Solomon wanted to influence Israel. Pastors and church leaders would love to have that kind of impact on their congregations.)

Pray together, thanking God for the opportunity He gives us to make a difference in other people's lives. Use the parts of Solomon's psalm that resonate most powerfully with you as you ask Him to guide and bless your efforts to bless others.

Suggested devotion from *The Love Languages Devotional Bible*, page 444 (Who Should Do What?)

FOR THE BIRDS

The theme of this adventure is birds—specifically, how God cares for even the smallest works of His creation, which are represented in the gospel of Matthew by birds. You'll find a flock of ideas for making the theme work for you.

30

GOING THE EXTRA MILE

The way to take this adventure to the next level would be to get up close and personal with birds. The best way to do that would be to visit a friend, family member, or acquaintance who keeps birds as pets.

Treat your visit as a fact-finding mission. Think of questions that you'd like to ask. Talk about the characteristics of different birds, including what they're like and how they show their personality. If you and the owner are comfortable with the idea, let a bird perch on your finger or shoulder.

MAKING IT WORK FOR YOU

The time and opportunities you have available will go a long way toward determining which bird-related activities you choose. Here are a few ideas to get you started.

▶ Build and paint a birdhouse together. Position it as close to a window as possible so that you can observe the comings and goings of various guests.

▶ Set up a bird feeder or birdbath in a place that offers a similar vantage point.

▶ Spend some time in a local bird preserve or nature sanctuary. See how many different species of birds you can photograph.

▶ Visit your local zoo. Spend time in the bird section. Talk to the zookeepers. Explore the interactive exhibits. Find out everything you've ever wanted to know about birds, from their eating habits to their aerodynamics.

▶ Watch a documentary about birds, such as *Winged Migration*, *March of the Penguins*, or *The Life of Birds*.

▶ Watch a feature-length movie that features birds, whether it's a live-action film such as *Fly Away Home* or *The Birds*, or an animated film such as *Rio*, *Happy Feet*, or *Legend of the Guardians: The Owls of Ga'Hoole*.

SPEAKING THE RIGHT LANGUAGE

If Receiving Gifts is the primary love language of your spouse, buy a souvenir that will serve as a reminder of your adventure: a stuffed bird. Give it a place of honor in your home. When you find yourselves struggling with worry or anxiety, bring it out and let it remind you of God's care and provision.

WEAVING THE THIRD STRAND

Read together Matthew 6:25–34. In the passage, Jesus assures His followers that God will provide for us. As evidence, He points to God's provision for smaller creatures:

> "Look at the birds of the air; they do not sow or reap or store away in barns, and yet your heavenly Father feeds them. Are you not much more valuable than they? Can any one of you by worrying add a single hour to your life?" (vv. 26–27).

Use the following questions as needed to guide your discussion of the passage. (Please note that the responses in parentheses are merely suggestions, ideas to stimulate your brainstorming and give you something to react to. They should not be viewed as the "correct" answers to the questions.)

▶ How does God care for the birds of the air? (He provides them with everything they need to survive. In addition to giving them wings to fly, He designed them to be able to withstand the elements. He gives them a plentiful food supply. He also "outfits" them with feathers, some of which are extraordinary.)

- ► What comfort can we take from Jesus' words? (If God lavishes such care on birds, He will certainly offer us no less. That means our worries are unfounded. No matter what situations we face, God will see us through.)

- ► If God cares for us, why do we face situations that make us uncomfortable or anxious about our well-being? (God doesn't promise us an easy life. That's not His will for us. He wants us to rely on Him, to trust in Him, to discover what He's capable of. That won't happen if everything goes just as we want it to.)

- ► What are your most common worries? (Some couples worry about finances. Others worry about health issues. Some worry about the well-being of their kids. Others worry about the well-being of their aging parents. The one thing all these worries have in common is that none of them is any match for God's strength.)

Pray together, thanking God for His care and provision for all creatures. Ask Him to remind you of Jesus' words in Matthew 6 when you are feeling anxious.

Suggested devotion from *The Love Languages Devotional Bible*, page 1041 (Financial Plans)

STARGAZERS

Spend an evening with your spouse enjoying the celestial wonders of the night sky.

31

GOING THE EXTRA MILE

Many universities have observatories that they open to the public. To prepare for your stargazing activity, schedule a visit to a local university observatory. You can learn the basics of astronomy from a professor (or a graduate student who gets paid to lead tours). If the tour offers time for questions and answers, you may be able to get some useful tips for planning your own stargazing adventure. At the very least, you'll walk away with a better understanding of what you'll be seeing in the night sky.

MAKING IT WORK FOR YOU

The key to making this activity work is to find the right location to do your stargazing. If you live in a city, light pollution may obscure your view of the night sky. Your best bet is to find a rural location, preferably someplace elevated and away from obstacles to your sight line.

Create a comfortable viewing area. You could use reclining beach chairs, positioned side by side, as well as pillows and blankets to make things cozy. Don't forget your favorite snacks and beverages—and perhaps a playlist of soothing instrumentals to help set the mood. You might also want to bring a flashlight with a red filter for illumination. The red filter allows you to see things without it affecting your ability to adapt to the darkness.

A telescope isn't necessary for an evening of casual stargazing. A pair of binoculars, however, can enhance the experience tremendously. Even a cheap pair of binoculars will allow you to see craters on the moon.

To get a sense of what you're looking at, you can print out a star chart (available online, if you prefer old-school technology) or download an app such as Night Sky, Stellarium, Star Walk, or Sky Map. Check the website of the American Meteor Society (amsmeteors.org) to find out when to schedule your stargazing for the best chance of seeing a meteor shower.

SPEAKING THE RIGHT LANGUAGE

If Receiving Gifts is your spouse's primary love language, you can offer a stellar present as part of this adventure. There are several online sites that offer the opportunity to name a star after your spouse.

(Unfortunately, the name won't officially be recognized by astronomers, but it's the thought that counts, isn't it?)

WEAVING THE THIRD STRAND

Read together Psalm 147:2–6:

> "The LORD builds up Jerusalem; he gathers the exiles of Israel. He heals the brokenhearted and binds up their wounds. He determines the number of the stars and calls them each by name. Great is our Lord and mighty in power; his understanding has no limit. The LORD sustains the humble but casts the wicked to the ground."

Use the following questions as needed to guide your discussion of the passage. (Please note that the responses in parentheses are merely suggestions, ideas to stimulate your brainstorming and give you something to react to. They should not be viewed as the "correct" answers to the questions.)

► Why do you think the psalmist praises God for His personal healing work in one verse and then for His limitless creation in the next? (Perhaps he's marveling at the fact that the One powerful enough to place the stars in the sky cares enough about individuals to tend to their suffering.)

► The psalmist referred to the stars in the sky to communicate the immensity of God's power. What image would you use? (Some people might refer to the mountains of the earth or the waters of the ocean.)

► What keeps us from fully appreciating God's power, as shown in His creation? (The distractions and busyness of everyday life can act as blinders, preventing us from appreciating the grand scope of our world. Also, familiarity tends to breed indifference. Seeing the same thing from the same perspective every day makes us lose sight of its awesome splendor.)

► How can we develop a God-honoring appreciation for the marvels of the physical world? (Paying attention is the key. We can put down our electronic devices, unplug from our headphones, and focus on the immensity of creation, as seen in the night sky, and the intricacy of creation, as seen in every living creature.)

Pray together, praising God for the immensity of His creation as well as for the personal attention He lavishes on each of us. Ask Him to help you maintain a spiritually healthy sense of awe and gratitude toward Him.

Suggested devotion from *The Love Languages Devotional Bible*, page 457 (Glory and Honor)

CRAFTY THINKING

If you've ever been to Vacation Bible School, you know just how fun craft time can be. Here's an opportunity to relive the experience as an adult, with your favorite person in the world working by your side.

32

GOING THE EXTRA MILE

You can take this adventure to the next level by co-ordinating your craft day with someone who needs craftwork done. For example, your church's drama team may need a backdrop painted or some sets built. Or perhaps someone you know is in need of a creative and inexpensive Halloween costume. If that's the case, you'll need to get the necessary information before you begin your project. Take your measurements, get input from the necessary people, and then get started.

MAKING IT WORK FOR YOU

A quick online search for craft projects will yield more results than you could sort through in a week. Are you interested in melting crayons to create candles? You'll find an easy-to-follow tutorial for it, as well as for everything else from creating a dream catcher to designing scrapbook pages.

You also could build and launch model rockets. You could create a sand art picture frame. You could do a paint by number. You could build a bird-house. If none of those ideas appeal to you, visit a hobby store. Chances are good that you'll find something that the two of you can do together.

With this adventure, the process is much more significant than the end product. Obviously, you'll want to create something that you're proud of. But much more important is the time you spend working together, talking together, teasing each other, and encouraging each other.

SPEAKING THE RIGHT LANGUAGE

This adventure sets up rather nicely for someone whose primary love language is Receiving Gifts.

The obvious thing to do would be to gift your spouse with your craft project when you finish it. A not-so-obvious thing to do would be to design the project with your spouse in mind—for example, using his or her favorite colors—and to explain what you're doing while you're doing it.

WEAVING THE THIRD STRAND

Read together Psalm 8:3–4:

"When I consider your heavens, the work of your fingers, the moon and the stars, which you have set in place, what is mankind that you are mindful of them, human beings that you care for them?"

Use the following questions as needed to guide your discussion of the passage. (Please note that the responses in parentheses are merely suggestions, ideas to stimulate your brainstorming and give you something to react to. They should not be viewed as the "correct" answers to the questions.)

▶ The psalmist mentioned the "heavens . . . the moon and the stars." If you were going to write your own psalm about God's creation, what would you be sure to mention? (Someone with a "macro" view might do as the psalmist did and express awe about the immensity of the universe. Someone with a "micro" view might focus on the intricate parts of the body, such as the eye or the brain. Still others might focus on the beauty of nature.)

▶ When you consider the entire scope of God's creation, how do you feel about yourself? (The reaction of the psalmist—to consider just how small you are in the grand scheme of things—is probably pretty normal. But it's also cause to feel especially blessed.)

▶ What does it mean that God is "mindful" of us? (Even in the big picture of the universe and everything in it,

He cares deeply about His personal relationship with each of us.)

▶ How does God show His care for us? (He sent His Son to die for us so we can live forever with Him. He answers our prayers. He calms our fears. He provides for our needs.)

Pray together, praising God for specific aspects of His creation. Spend some time with this. If you're feeling creative, turn your prayer into a psalm—perhaps one modeled after Psalm 8. Ask God to help you remember that He is mindful of you and that He cares for you—especially when you're facing difficult circumstances.

Suggested devotion from *The Love Languages Devotional Bible*, page 230 (Dear God)

GRAFFITI ARTISTS

HAPPY BIRTHDAY

GOING THE EXTRA MILE

You can go the extra mile with this adventure by coordinating it with a special event in someone's life. A graduation, an engagement, a new job, the birth of a baby, or even just a birthday or anniversary could be used as justification for the graffiti treatment.

The more personalized your handiwork is, the more likely it is to be appreciated. So do some research and find out if there are any special events coming up in people's lives that might be cause for a graffiti greeting.

MAKING IT WORK FOR YOU

The key to making this adventure work is to choose the right person's home to decorate. Obviously, it will need to be someone with a sense of humor, an appreciation of graffiti art, and a tolerance for some temporary messiness. The ideal candidate will be someone who's out of town, or at least away for a few hours, giving you time to work.

Using sidewalk chalk, which is available in a wide array of colors, decorate the driveway or porch. Write a fun message. Draw a football helmet, team logo, graduation mortarboard, or any other appropriate symbols to reflect the person's interests or the events going on in his or her life. Draw a caricature of the person —or of yourselves. Or come up with your own design.

Use your best judgment with this adventure. Be sensitive to any homeowner's association rules. Also be ready to wash away your handiwork when you're done.

SPEAKING THE RIGHT LANGUAGE

If Quality Time is your spouse's primary love language, you can make this adventure special by talking together about the pranks you pulled when you were younger. Encourage your spouse to share some of the harmless (and perhaps not so harmless) things he or she did as a teenager. Share some stories of your own. Talk about any regrets you may have. Talk also about strategies for keeping your kids from making the type of wrong choices that you made.

WEAVING THE THIRD STRAND

Read together Exodus 35:30–35:

Then Moses said to the Israelites, "See, the LORD has chosen Bezalel son of Uri, the son of Hur, of the tribe of Judah, and he has filled him with the Spirit of God, with wisdom, with understanding, with knowledge and with all kinds of skills—to make artistic designs for work in gold, silver and bronze, to cut and set stones, to work in wood and to engage in all kinds of artistic crafts. And he has given both him and Oholiab son of Ahisamak, of the tribe of Dan, the ability to teach others. He has filled them with skill to do all kinds of work as engravers, designers, embroiderers in blue, purple and scarlet yarn and fine linen, and weavers—all of them skilled workers and designers."

Use the following questions as needed to guide your discussion of the passage. (Please note that the responses in parentheses are merely suggestions, ideas to stimulate your brainstorming and give you something to react to. They should not be viewed as the "correct" answers to the questions.)

▶ What does God reveal about Himself in this passage? (He is a lover of beauty. He appreciates craftsmanship. He encourages artistic expression. He could have instructed workers just to build something functional and plain. Instead, He enlisted skilled artisans—people He had gifted specially for such a purpose.)

▶ In what ways did the Lord bless Bezalel? (God filled Bezalel with His Spirit. He gave him wisdom, understanding, and knowledge. He gave him skills to create artistic designs using a variety of materials, including gold, silver, bronze, precious stones, and wood. He also gave Bezalel the ability to teach his artistry to others.)

- ▶ Why is creative expression so important? (It's part of being made in the image of the Creator.)

- ▶ What's your favorite way to express yourself creatively? (You don't have to be an artist to use artistic gifts, whether it's writing, singing, painting, drawing, or creating crafts.)

Pray together, thanking God for His gift of artistry. Ask Him to open your eyes to the artistic beauty that surrounds you. Ask Him also to help you express yourself creatively and artistically for His glory.

Suggested devotion from *The Love Languages Devotional Bible*, page 353 (Faithful to the End)

EYESORE NO MORE

Find a spot in your community that could use some sprucing up. Spend an afternoon with your spouse beautifying the area. Unwind in the great outdoors while you make a difference in your community.

34

GOING THE EXTRA MILE

For the purposes of this book, this adventure is a one-time thing—a way to spend some time unwinding with your spouse. For the purposes of your community, you may want to make it a regular part of your monthly calendar. Set aside some time each month to maintain your adopted site. After you've done the heavy lifting the first time, your subsequent cleanups will likely be much easier and quicker.

You might also become an advocate for adopting sites to clean up among your friends and family. If enough people follow your lead, you may make a very real difference in your community.

MAKING IT WORK FOR YOU

Many state highway systems offer the opportunity for groups and individuals to "adopt" sections of the roadway. They assume responsibility for keeping their assigned areas free of garbage and debris. On some road systems, you can find small signs that tell you who is responsible for keeping that segment of the roadside clean.

This adventure offers a twist on the adopt-a-highway program. You and your spouse will "adopt" an area to clean up. Your options are virtually limitless. Is there an underpass near you where the garbage and debris from the highway collect? Is there an abandoned house with an overgrown lawn and empty bottles strewn everywhere? Is there a nearby creek or waterway where people illegally dump their garbage? Is there an area of your local park in need of upkeep?

Whatever you choose to tackle, make sure you're prepared. You'll need gloves, garbage bags, and maybe a trash picker. For certain bigger jobs, you may need a lawn mower, a weed trimmer, and perhaps even a pickup truck to haul away garbage. In your zeal to choose a location and get started, make sure you don't trespass on private property.

SPEAKING THE RIGHT LANGUAGE

If Acts of Service is the primary love language of your spouse, you can make this adventure special by anticipating his or her needs. Create a playlist of your spouse's favorite songs to listen to while you work. Stock a small cooler with your spouse's favorite beverage. Make a food run to your spouse's favorite local restaurant. While you're both doing something thoughtful for your community, you can do something thoughtful for your spouse.

WEAVING THE THIRD STRAND

Read together the following passages:

▶ Genesis 2:15: "The LORD God took the man and put him in the Garden of Eden to work it and take care of it."

▶ Numbers 35:33: "Do not pollute the land where you are."

Use the following questions as needed to guide your discussion of the passages. (Please note that the responses in parentheses are merely suggestions, ideas to stimulate your brainstorming and give you something to react to. They should not be viewed as the "correct" answers to the questions.)

▶ What do you think Adam and Eve's responsibilities in the Garden of Eden involved? (They likely tended to the plants and animals as needed. Perhaps they planted and harvested. They served as caretakers of God's creation.)

▶ Why do you think work plays such a large role in God's plan for us? (He established the cycle of work and rest in the seven days of creation. Our capacity for work is part of our being created in God's image. God designed us to find a sense of satisfaction, accomplishment, and fulfillment in our work.)

► Why do you think God instructed the Israelites not to pollute their land? (Their land was a gift from God—something He had promised their ancestors. He wanted them to treat it with a sense of responsibility and reverence.)

► What is our responsibility today as caretakers of God's creation? (Many environmental problems seem too big to be handled by individuals. But we can start by caring for our immediate surroundings. Though it may seem like a drop in a bucket, God will bless our efforts.)

Pray together, thanking God for the beauty of His creation and for entrusting you (along with the entire human race) with the responsibility of caring for it. Ask Him to bless and multiply your efforts to beautify your community.

Suggested devotion from *The Love Languages Devotional Bible*, page 143 (Faithful Stewards)

DID YOU KNOW?

If you have an hour or so to unwind, play "Did You Know?" with your spouse. Take turns sharing information with each other that you think your partner may not know. See how many new things you can learn, whether they involve pop culture, history, science—or something more personal.

35

GOING THE EXTRA MILE

If you want to put a little extra effort into this adventure, share your "Did You Know?" facts in question form. Create a fun quiz for your spouse, using true-false or multiple-choice questions. For example, you might ask, "True or false? Nine different cities have been the capital of the United States." (True.) Or you might ask, "Which of these cities has not been the capital of the United States: New York, Boston, Baltimore, or Philadelphia?" (Boston.)

MAKING IT WORK FOR YOU

Even if you and your spouse are both *Jeopardy!*-level know-it-alls, you should be able to find plenty of "new" things to share with each other. You can start with trivia. Take turns sharing some of the most unusual and obscure facts you can find about . . . well, any subject, from abstract expressionism to zoological classifications.

But you don't have to confine yourselves to trivia. You could also draw on personal experiences that you've never shared with your spouse before. Talk about the events surrounding your first kiss, your most embarrassing moment, your most significant brush with a celebrity, or your favorite food when you were a kid—anything that might cover new ground, as far as your spouse is concerned.

If you're ready for the adventure to take a deeper turn, you could talk about even more intensely personal things. You might share feelings you've never talked about before. You might admit to fears that your spouse is unaware of. You might talk about the "little," seemingly insignificant things that bring you joy.

Even if your adventure lasts no more than an hour or so, there's a good chance that you and your spouse will come away from it with an enhanced knowledge of—and perhaps even an enhanced appreciation for—each other.

SPEAKING THE RIGHT LANGUAGE

If Words of Affirmation is your spouse's primary love language, you have an opportunity to make this adventure resonate in a special way. Focus your "Did You Know?" facts on your spouse. For example, you might say something like, "Did you know that the first time I saw you my mouth literally dropped open?" or "Did you know that the sound of your breathing at night is soothing to me?"

WEAVING THE THIRD STRAND

Read together Proverbs 1:5:

"Let the wise listen and add to their learning,
and let the discerning get guidance."

Use the following questions as needed to guide your discussion of the passage. (Please note that the responses in parentheses are merely suggestions, ideas to stimulate your brainstorming and give you something to react to. They should not be viewed as the "correct" answers to the questions.)

► What's the difference between knowledge and wisdom? (Knowledge is an awareness of facts, an ability to come up with a "right" answer. Wisdom is the ability to apply knowledge in a beneficial, God-honoring way.)

► Why should the wise listen? (The wiser you are, the more aware you are of how much more you have to learn. Proverbs 16:18 tells us that pride goes before destruction, a haughty spirit before a fall. When you become convinced that people have nothing to teach you, your wisdom suffers.)

► How do wise people know who to listen to? (Under the right circumstances, anyone can be a teacher.

So, a wise person always listens with an open mind, considers the source, considers the circumstances, and then weighs a person's words carefully. If the wise person finds truth in those words, his or her wisdom is increased.)

► How do you decide whether you'll follow certain guidance? (The best strategy is to pray about it—to seek wisdom from the Lord.)

Pray together, thanking God for the opportunities you have to increase your learning, understanding, discernment, and wisdom every day. Ask Him to guide your decision-making so that it reflects His wisdom and accomplishes His will.

Suggested devotion from *The Love Languages Devotional Bible*, page 520 (In God We Trust)

A HOMETOWN TOUR

36

Lead your spouse on a tour of your hometown. Point out the places that loom large in your childhood, from your family home to the site of your first kiss to the first place you ever worked. Bring your favorite stories to life by giving your spouse a glimpse of where they took place.

GOING THE EXTRA MILE

You (or your spouse, depending on whose hometown you choose) can make this adventure special by embracing your role as tour guide. You can pique your spouse's curiosity by creating an itinerary that teases the things he or she will see. For example, you might list something like "Monkey Bars, Playground, Edgewood Elementary School—see the exact location where I knocked out my two front teeth!" or "The skate return desk at Roller-Rama, where the girl I liked told me that she was going to prom with my best friend."

You can keep things light with a tongue-in-cheek approach while still highlighting some of the events that marked your formative years, for better or worse.

MAKING IT WORK FOR YOU

Here's the ideal scenario for this adventure. You and your spouse grew up in different towns. You didn't know each other. All you know about each other's hometowns is what you've heard from stories. This adventure offers an opportunity to put faces, names, and places to those stories.

Your first order of business is to choose which hometown to visit. If the one you choose is relatively close, you can pull off this adventure in an afternoon. If not, you may need to plan a road trip.

The adventure itself will be a glorified tour of the town—one that focuses not on historical sites or popular points of interest but on places that played key roles in your childhood. The obvious place to start is your childhood home. Your tour might also include stops at your elementary school, the fast-food restaurant where you worked, and your favorite hangouts. Your goal is to give your spouse a sense of what life was like for you there.

SPEAKING THE RIGHT LANGUAGE

If your spouse is the one going back to his or her hometown—and if your spouse's primary love language is Quality Time—you can make your adventure extra special by preparing some questions beforehand. You've likely heard enough stories about your spouse's childhood to be able to ask some relevant questions ("Where did your brother push you off your bike?").

The right questions will confirm for your spouse that you listen to and care about his or her stories. They'll also inspire the kind of conversation from which quality time is made.

WEAVING THE THIRD STRAND

Read together Proverbs 22:6:

"Start children off on the way they should go, and
even when they are old they will not turn from it."

Use the following questions as needed to guide your discussion of the passage. (Please note that the responses in parentheses are merely suggestions, ideas to stimulate your brainstorming and give you something to react to. They should not be viewed as the "correct" answers to the questions.)

▶ How did your parents "start you off"? (At one end of the spectrum are parents who raise their kids in strict households, with a lot of rules and discipline. At the other end are parents who raise their kids in permissive households, with few rules and little discipline. Talk about where you fit in relation to those two extremes.)

▶ What are some values that were instilled in you by your hometown? (Some people might recall being taught that nothing is more important than family. Others might remember being told that neighbors help neighbors. Other values might include hard work, honesty, faithfulness, patriotism, and service.)

- ▶ Give some examples of how those values have stayed with you as an adult. (Perhaps the emphasis your parents or others placed on hard work rubbed off on you to the point that you tend to judge people's character based on how hard they work.)

- ▶ What specific steps have you taken to "start your children off on the way they should go"? (Possibilities might include anything from making family prayer and Bible study priorities to setting strict guidelines for social media to sharing openly and honestly about the mistakes you made when you were younger.)

Pray together, thanking the Lord for the godly influences in your life, whether they came from your parents, grandparents, or others. Ask Him to bless your efforts to be a source of wisdom to your children and others.

Suggested devotion from *The Love Languages Devotional Bible*, page 85 (Are You Honorable?)

THE SUBJECT IS APPLES

Can you build a fun and relaxing day around a single random theme? Here's your chance to find out. The theme is apples. What can you do with it?

37

GOING THE EXTRA MILE

The obvious ideal location for this adventure is an apple orchard. If you live within driving distance of an orchard, plan a trip there. The closer to peak season you schedule your trip, the more productive your adventure will be. Naturally, your primary objective is to pick apples. But instead of loading up on your favorite variety (such as Honeycrisp), try picking a couple of apples from as many different varieties as you can find. That way, you can take them home and do a taste test. Who knows? You may find a new favorite.

Many orchards offer other things to do as well, including corn mazes and hayrides. You'll probably also want to spend some time in the orchard store, stocking up on everything apple—from butter to cider to pie.

MAKING IT WORK FOR YOU

If a visit to an apple orchard is out of the question, you can still have fun in any number of ways that touch on the theme of apples. If you have a well-stocked farmers market or produce section at your local grocery, you can still do a taste test. Buy as many different varieties of apples as you can find and take them home to sample.

If you find a variety that would be just right for baking, you could make an apple pie together. It's up to you whether you use an old family recipe or try something new.

If you have an artistic bent, you could do some apple carving. If you do an online search for "apple carving," you'll find all kinds of ideas to inspire you. You could try juggling apples. You could have apple-seed-spitting contests—for accuracy and for distance. You could even play the game Apples to Apples. Anything that involves apples is fair game.

SPEAKING THE RIGHT LANGUAGE

If Physical Touch is the primary love language of your spouse, you can make this adventure special by incorporating some physical challenges that lend themselves to plenty of touching. One option is to work together to try to move apples from, say, your kitchen counter to your dining room table—without using your hands.

WEAVING THE THIRD STRAND

To continue your "fruit" theme, read together Matthew 7:15–20. In the passage, Jesus warns His followers to avoid false prophets. He points out that the way to recognize false prophets is to look at their actions. "A good tree cannot bear bad fruit, and a bad tree cannot bear good fruit. . . . Thus, by their fruit you will recognize them" (vv. 18, 20).

Use the following questions as needed to guide your discussion of the passage. (Please note that the responses in parentheses are merely suggestions, ideas to stimulate your brainstorming and give you something to react to. They should not be viewed as the "correct" answers to the questions.)

► Why are fruits so important in determining a person's character? (When it comes to the Christian faith, "talking the talk" means nothing if you don't "walk the walk.")

► What kind of fruits is Jesus talking about? (In Galatians 5:22–23, the apostle Paul lists nine qualities that he refers to as "the fruit of the Spirit." They are "love, joy, peace, forbearance, kindness, goodness, faithfulness, gentleness and self-control.")

► Isn't it possible for people to fake having fruit? (It may be possible to fool people for a while, especially those who fail to use discernment. Eventually, though, a person's true nature—and spiritual barrenness—will reveal itself.)

- ► How can we keep from getting fooled? (The best strategy is to pray for discernment and to look for actual fruit.)

- ► How can you make sure that people see the fruit of the Spirit in your life? (We can work hard to live an authentic life in Christ, to allow people to see us "warts and all," so there's no temptation to put up a front. We can ask for God's guidance and wisdom in every situation we face.)

Pray together, thanking God for the wisdom of His Word. Ask Him to give you discernment when people claim to speak for God. Ask His Holy Spirit to help you recognize false messages. Ask Him also to bless your efforts to yield fruit in your own life.

Suggested devotion from *The Love Languages Devotional Bible*, page 542 (The Value of a Legacy)

SHELTER ANGELS

Volunteer at your local animal shelter. Donate your time and energy to helping animals in need of care.

38

GOING THE EXTRA MILE

Going the extra mile for this adventure would involve fostering a pet. If you think that's something you want to do, you'll need to make arrangements before the day of your adventure. Many pet fostering agencies require applicants to do a phone interview and complete on-line training before they release a pet into their care. By making the necessary arrangements beforehand, you'll be able to take home your foster pet at the end of your adventure.

MAKING IT WORK FOR YOU

In order to schedule a volunteer date that works for you, you'll need to contact your local shelter well in advance. Some shelters try to discourage one-time volunteering. They prefer potential volunteers to make a commitment to working at the shelter for a certain number of hours each week. Some shelters may waive that commitment if the need for volunteers is great.

You and your spouse will get to spend time with the animals in the shelter, but you should also be prepared to do other types of work as well. Depending on the shelter's needs, you may be asked to clean cages, stack bags of food, interact with people looking to adopt a pet, or run errands.

If you and your spouse have a chance to interact with each other while you're volunteering, talk about your favorite pets from childhood. What were their names? What were they like? What do you miss most about them? You might also talk about your "dream pet"—the animal or breed you've always wanted as a pet.

SPEAKING THE RIGHT LANGUAGE

If Acts of Service is the primary love language of your cat- or dog-loving spouse, you can demonstrate your love in a very real way by assuming primary responsibility for the foster pet in your home. That may involve anything from creating a comfortable space for your foster pet to ensure it's properly fed to administering medication to cleaning up after it. By doing the actual work of fostering a pet, you'll free up your spouse to enjoy his or her time with your furry visitor.

WEAVING THE THIRD STRAND

Read together the following passages:

▶ Genesis 1:21: "So God created the great creatures of the sea and every living thing with which the water teems and that moves about in it, according to their kinds, and every winged bird according to its kind. And God saw that it was good."

▶ Luke 12:6: "Are not five sparrows sold for two pennies? Yet not one of them is forgotten by God."

▶ Proverbs 12:10: "The righteous care for the needs of their animals, but the kindest acts of the wicked are cruel."

Use the following questions as needed to guide your discussion of the passages. (Please note that the responses in parentheses are merely suggestions, ideas to stimulate your brainstorming and give you something to react to. They should not be viewed as the "correct" answers to the questions.)

▶ Based on the creation account of Genesis 1:21, what is the most basic reason for us to care for animals? (God created them. All animals are His handiwork. For that reason alone, they are deserving of our care and attention.)

▶ How is that point driven home in the final sentence of verse 21? ("God saw that it was good." He took special delight in the animals He had created.)

► In Luke 12, Jesus urges His followers not to worry because God cares for our needs. What does His reference to sparrows in verse 6 reveal about God's nature? (His concern for the creatures He made didn't end at creation. He is aware of—and cares for—every individual bird, animal, and human.)

► Why do you think the writer of Proverbs used caring for the needs of animals as evidence of righteousness? (To care for someone or something who can do nothing for you is Christlike behavior. It's also evidence of our being created in God's image. After all, He cares for us when we can do absolutely nothing for Him.)

Pray together, thanking God for creating such lovable animals. Ask Him to bless your efforts to care for the animals in your home and in your community.

Suggested devotion from *The Love Languages Devotional Bible*, page 1257 (Fix Your Thoughts)

ALL-NIGHTER

39

When was the last time you stayed up all night—on purpose? Here's a chance to relive the carefree days (and nights) of your youth by not going to bed until the sun comes up.

GOING THE EXTRA MILE

Unless you and your spouse are night owls by nature, you may need to do a little preparation for your all-night adventure. Your best strategy is to take a long nap in the afternoon, if your schedule allows for such a luxury. Even a quick catnap could help you stay up a little later.

Caffeine will also be your friend throughout the day. If you've ever wanted to pour yourself a cup of coffee after dinner but were afraid it would keep you up all night, here's your chance to indulge. Have two—it's going to be a long night. If you're not a fan of java, try some tea, chocolate, soda, energy drinks, or energy bars. Just don't overdo it.

Another strategy is to stay active. Alternate sedentary activities with short walks or quick workouts—anything to get the blood and adrenaline flowing.

MAKING IT WORK FOR YOU

An all-nighter offers a world of opportunities. You and your spouse could do a movie marathon. You could watch an entire series (Star Wars or The Lord of the Rings, for example) or alternate your favorite movies. If you're feeling more active, you could work out at a twenty-four-hour gym. You could go shopping at a twenty-four-hour grocery. You could make a late night/early morning doughnut run. If you live in a safe neighborhood, you could go for a midnight stroll—or a 2:00 a.m. run, for that matter.

Try a combination of activities. Cap your adventure by watching the sunrise together. After that, you're free to crash.

During your adventure, talk about times when you stayed up all night in the past. How old were you the first time you did it? What's the longest you've ever gone without sleep? What effect did it have on you? What are your favorite memories from sleepovers that turned into all-nighters? How many times did you pull all-nighters in college during final exams?

SPEAKING THE RIGHT LANGUAGE

If your spouse's primary love language is Acts of Service, you can do something special for him or her by anticipating the aftermath of your all-nighter. Make arrangements to clear your spouse's schedule for the following day. Volunteer to take the kids where they need to go or run other errands. Post a "Do Not Disturb" sign on your bedroom door. Give your spouse an opportunity to catch up on his or her sleep.

WEAVING THE THIRD STRAND

Read together some Bible passages that involve sleep. Here are a few to get you started:

- ► Mark 5:21–24, 35–43

- ► Matthew 8:23–27

- ► Proverbs 3:24

- ► Proverbs 6:9–11

Aside from the key subject, the passages aren't really linked in any way. But they can spur some interesting conversation about God's Word. Depending on how many passages you choose to read together, use one or more of the following questions to guide your discussion. (Please note that the responses in parentheses are merely suggestions, ideas to stimulate your brainstorming and give you something to react to. They should not be viewed as the "correct" answers to the questions.)

- ► For Mark 5:21–24, 35–43: Why do you think Jesus used the word "asleep" to describe the dead girl's condition? (As Jesus proved after His crucifixion, death—like sleep—is a temporary state, one that can and will be interrupted.)

- ► For Matthew 8:23–27: What do you take away from the fact that Jesus was sleeping through the storm that threatened to capsize the boat? (Jesus knew what the disciples didn't—that the storm was no match for His power. As a result, everyone under His care was safe from its ravages. He had no reason to worry about the squall, so He slept.)

► For Proverbs 3:24: The writer is talking about wisdom in this passage. How does wisdom ease our minds and give us sleep that's "sweet"? (Wisdom allows us to see God's work in the difficult areas of our lives. It gives us a healthy perspective on our problems, pain, and anything else that might trouble our sleep.)

► For Proverbs 6:9–11: When does sleep become counter-productive? (People who work when they should be sleeping pose a threat to their health. Those who sleep when they should be working open themselves up to accusations of laziness.)

Pray together, thanking God for the gift that makes all others possible—that is, for allowing you to wake from your sleep and experience a new day. Ask Him to help you make the most of your day—to wring every blessing and every opportunity from it—so that you may enjoy His gift of restful sleep.

Suggested devotion from *The Love Languages Devotional Bible*, page 1332 (First Love)

AN 1800 KIND OF DAY

Here's an opportunity to demonstrate your heartiness, your ingenuity, and your pioneer spirit. Plan a day that simulates what life was like before people had automobiles, phones, or electricity. See how well you can do without modern conveniences.

40

GOING THE EXTRA MILE

A little research will go a long way toward making this adventure meaningful. A few quick online searches will give you a pretty good idea of how people spent their time in 1800. If you're serious about maintaining the integrity of the adventure, find out what pastimes were popular back then, what songs people sang, and other information that will help you replicate life at the turn of the nineteenth century.

MAKING IT WORK FOR YOU

Your adventure is to live like pioneers for a day. That means, unless you have a horse and wagon, any traveling you do must be done by foot. It also means that you'll need to use candles or lanterns for lighting and a fireplace (or an outdoor firepit) for

cooking. Depending on how far you want to take the adventure, you might also choose to eat only food that would have been available to people in 1800.

One option is to coordinate this adventure with a day in the garden. If you have plans to plant, weed, or harvest, make sure you use only tools and implements that were used in 1800. And

nothing says "1800" like pulling vegetables from your garden to cook for dinner that night.

SPEAKING THE RIGHT LANGUAGE

If you choose to embark on this adventure when the temperature is chilly, you'll need to improvise methods for keeping warm inside your house.

(Homes in 1800 did not have central heating.) This is good news for someone whose primary love language is Physical Touch. In addition to sleeping near the fireplace, you and your spouse will need to use body heat to stay cozy and warm.

WEAVING THE THIRD STRAND

Read together Luke 16:10–15. Use the following questions as needed to guide your discussion of the passage. (Please note that the responses in parentheses are merely suggestions, ideas to stimulate your brainstorming and give you something to react to. They should not be viewed as the "correct" answers to the questions.)

- In these verses Jesus speaks of money as something God entrusts to us. What difference does it make to view money this way rather than as our possession? (We must look to God for direction on how to use everything He has entrusted to us. Spending time in prayer each day—listening for His wisdom and direction—will help guide us in the decisions we make about money and material possessions.)

- How would your life be different if you treated money and possessions as gifts entrusted to you by God? (Perhaps you would be more generous, be less burdened with the care of your things, and have more time for the care of yourself and others.)

- How are these verses about living faithfully for God? (Those things that would stand in the way of a faithful relationship with God must be put in their appropriate place. True faithfulness to God requires life in Him to be our ultimate priority. Nothing else can supersede that.)

Pray together, thanking God for His faithfulness. Ask Him to help you set aside distractions and the priorities of the world in order to fully embrace the life He offers.

Suggested devotion from *The Love Languages Devotional Bible*, page 1318 (Cleansing)

TRUTH OR DARE

The game that's spiced up countless teenage parties can now be an adventure for you and your spouse. You can wind down in the comfort of your own home with a few rounds of Truth or Dare.

41

GOING THE EXTRA MILE

Talk to some of your spouse's childhood friends—people he or she may have played Truth or Dare with in the past. See if they have any recollections of truths or dares that you could reference in your own game.

If they can't remember any specific truths or dares, ask for some information you can use. Did your spouse have a secret childhood crush? Is there an embarrassing story that involves your spouse? Have some fun with the information you get by turning them into "truths" for your game.

If you can't talk to your spouse's childhood friends, his or her siblings or parents may be able to supply the information you're looking for.

MAKING IT WORK FOR YOU

The secret to success with Truth or Dare is coming up with the right questions and the right dares. Here are a few ideas to get you started.

TRUTHS

▶ What's the most embarrassing thing that's ever happened to you?

▶ What's the most childish thing that you still do?

▶ What's the most awkward date you ever had?

DARES

▶ Let me style your hair any way I want, take a picture of the results, and post it on social media.

▶ Swallow a spoonful of mustard.

▶ Dance without music for one minute.

SPEAKING THE RIGHT LANGUAGE

If Acts of Service is your spouse's primary love language, you can make this adventure special by organizing a reunion with one or more of his or her old friends—the ones your spouse may have played Truth or Dare with in the past.

WEAVING THE THIRD STRAND

Read together Ephesians 4:15:

"Instead, speaking the truth in love, we will grow
to become in every respect the mature body of him
who is the head, that is, Christ."

Use the following questions as needed to guide your
discussion of the passage. (Please note that the responses in
parentheses are merely suggestions, ideas to stimulate your
brainstorming and give you something to react to. They should
not be viewed as the "correct" answers to the questions.)

► When is it most difficult to tell the truth? (In some
cases, it's difficult to be honest when the truth will make
us look bad or change someone's opinion of us. In other
cases, it's difficult to be honest with someone when you
don't know how that person will react.)

► What's the difference between speaking the truth and
speaking the truth in love? (People who simply speak
the truth usually call it brutal honesty. And while the
"honesty" part is admirable, the "brutal" part can do
more damage than good. When you speak the truth in
love, your goal is not to punish or embarrass someone
but to seek the best for him or her.)

► Why is it important to speak the truth in love? (Passages
such as 1 John 4:19 make it clear that love should be at
the center of everything we do as followers of Christ. We
show love to others because God first showed love to us.)

▶ Why is it important to establish a reputation as someone who can be counted on to speak the truth in love? (Insincere compliments and thoughtless encouragement are easy to find on social media. A friend who genuinely has your best interests at heart—and who isn't afraid to lovingly tell you things that you may not want to hear— is a rarity. If you can become such a rarity in someone else's life, you'll have the opportunity to exert a godly influence.)

▶ What's the best strategy for speaking the truth in love? (Knowing how best to communicate with the person is essential. If you can use the person's primary love language, you have a better chance of speaking truth in a way that resonates.)

Pray together, thanking God for the people in your life who will speak the truth to you in love. Ask Him to bless your efforts to be lovingly truthful with the people in your life so that they will recognize you as someone who can be trusted.

Suggested devotion from *The Love Languages Devotional Bible*, page 1231 (Captive Thoughts)

AS GOOD AS YOU REMEMBER

> Relive some of your favorite things from childhood with your spouse. Try to remember what made them special all those years ago and see if their charms still hold up for you as adults.

42

GOING THE EXTRA MILE

One way to take this adventure to the next level would be to visit the place where you or your spouse grew up. Go to the playground or the Little League field where you used to play. Marvel at how much smaller everything seems now. Check out the local mall where you used to hang out. Visit the candy store or ice-cream stand that you remember from your childhood.

Another option would be to order vintage candy—the kind you and your spouse grew up loving but can no longer find in stores. You can find several vintage candy sites online.

MAKING IT WORK FOR YOU

This adventure lends itself to a variety of options. At the easy end of the spectrum, you could watch a favorite movie from childhood while you eat your favorite snacks from childhood. You could play a favorite childhood board game or video game. You and your spouse could read each other's favorite books from childhood.

The key to this adventure is not so much the activity you choose as it is the memories and nostalgia that are inspired by it. Keep a running commentary throughout your adventure of what you remember about the movie, snack, game, or whatever else you choose to indulge in. Why did it appeal to you so much? What feelings does it bring  up? What do you remember about the first time you experienced it? Afterward, talk about your reactions to it now. Is it still as good or as enjoyable as you remember? If so, what do you think that says about you? If not, how does it make you feel to know that you've "grown out of it"?

SPEAKING THE RIGHT LANGUAGE

If Acts of Service is the primary love language of your spouse, you can do something special for him or her by reviving an old hobby or celebrating an old interest. For example, let's say your spouse had a collection of baseball cards that he stored in an old shoe-box. You could put those cards in a display album and have them appraised by an expert. Or, let's say your spouse had a box full of old gymnastics trophies. You could build a shelf for them in your basement.

 ## WEAVING THE THIRD STRAND

Read together 1 Corinthians 13:11:

> "When I was a child, I talked like a child, I thought like a child, I reasoned like a child. When I became a man, I put the ways of childhood behind me."

Use the following questions as needed to guide your discussion of the passage. (Please note that the responses in parentheses are merely suggestions, ideas to stimulate your brainstorming and give you something to react to. They should not be viewed as the "correct" answers to the questions.)

- ▶ When you read Paul's words "When I was a child . . . I thought like a child," what comes to mind? What were some of the childish things you believed when you were younger? (Perhaps you thought the sun and the moon were the same thing. Or that superheroes were real. Or that your mom and dad were the smartest people in the world.)

- ▶ What are some fears that you had as a child? (Many kids have a fear of the dark—or of something happening to their parents. Some kids, due to particular circumstances, may develop a fear of sharks, clowns, heights, crowds, or any number of other things.)

- When did you start to put away childish things? (For many kids, that time comes when they start school. Peers have a not-so-subtle way of correcting childish thinking.)

- What childish things have been hardest for you to put away? (Competitiveness might fall into that category for a lot of people. The need to always be right is another possibility.)

- When you compare your Christian faith now with your childhood faith, what differences do you see? (On the positive side, you probably understand difficult theological concepts a little better. Your experiences likely have deepened your faith. On the negative side, your childish wonder and enthusiasm likely have diminished over the years.)

Pray together, thanking God for the spiritual maturity you see in yourself and in your spouse. Ask Him to bless your continuing efforts to put childish things behind you and grow in your Christian faith.

Suggested devotion from *The Love Languages Devotional Bible*, page 995
(A Forgiving Spirit)

10,000 STEPS (x2)

The only things you'll need for this adventure are a couple of fitness trackers (or pedometers, if you're old school), a pair of quality walking shoes for each of you, and a can-do attitude. Your goal is to take 10,000 steps apiece.

43

GOING THE EXTRA MILE

You can add an element of challenge to your adventure by thinking in terms of exact increments. For example, you might go to a mall and stay until you've taken, say, 2,000 steps. But you'll need to coordinate it so that the 2,000th step for each of you is the last one you take before you get in your car. Likewise, you might also coordinate your day so that the 10,000th step for each of you is the last one you take before you get into bed.

MAKING IT WORK FOR YOU

There are countless conventional and unconventional ways to get your steps in. Here are a few ideas to get you started.

- If you have a dog, make it your goal to wear him out with the kind of walk he dreams about—one that doesn't end with a loop around the block but keeps going into areas he's never sniffed before. If you don't have a dog, volunteer to walk one of your neighbors' pets—preferably an energetic puppy.

- If you go shopping, park at the most distant space in the lot. Leave the good parking spaces for people who aren't trying to get 10,000 steps in.

- Dance—whether it's in a club or in your family room. Get your steps in while rhythmically moving with your spouse. If you prefer a video game prompt, you could play Dance Dance Revolution or some other game that involves dance steps.

- Make reservations at the highest rooftop restaurant in your area. Take the stairs instead of the elevator—before and after the meal.

- Guess the number of steps it will take to complete a trail in your local forest preserve. Then walk the trail to see whose guess was closer.

Work together and encourage each other throughout your adventure. Don't let it become a competition. As much as possible, try to take your 10,000 steps together.

SPEAKING THE RIGHT LANGUAGE

If Acts of Service is the primary love language of your spouse, you can demonstrate love in a profound and practical way. Before you embark on a day of walking, prepare a small backpack for your spouse. Fill it with energy bars, a water bottle, bug spray, sunscreen, a hat, and any other necessities you can think of. Make sure your spouse is ready for anything.

WEAVING THE THIRD STRAND

Read together 1 Corinthians 6:19–20:

> "Do you not know that your bodies are temples of the Holy Spirit, who is in you, whom you have received from God? You are not your own; you were bought at a price. Therefore honor God with your bodies."

Use the following questions as needed to guide your discussion of the passage. (Please note that the responses in parentheses are merely suggestions, ideas to stimulate your brainstorming and give you something to react to. They should not be viewed as the "correct" answers to the questions.)

- ▶ Why do you think the apostle Paul refers to our bodies as "temples of the Holy Spirit"? (As Christians, we have the Holy Spirit dwelling within us. Our bodies are His home.)

- ▶ Why are we not our own? (As Christians, we've given our lives to Jesus. We've surrendered control. Our wants and desires are secondary to His will. The good news for us is that He will do more with our lives than we ever could.)

▶ What was the "price" that was paid? (The price was the sacrificial death of Jesus Christ. He gave His life so we can have eternal life.)

▶ How do we honor God with our bodies? (We treat them like the gifts they are. We honor the One who dwells within us by caring for His temple. We take excellent care of our health so we are ready for any kind of service to God.)

Pray together, thanking God for the health you enjoy. Ask Him to bless your efforts to treat your body as a temple.

Suggested devotion from *The Love Languages Devotional Bible*, page 48 (The Sanctity of Sex)

THE BUILDUP

If this adventure were a meal, it would be approximately 75 percent appetizer and 25 percent entrée. Schedule a date with your spouse—a relaxing, romantic getaway. Then work together to build anticipation for the date—so much so that the buildup becomes the adventure.

44

GOING THE EXTRA MILE

Enlist your friends and family to help you build anticipation for your date. Arrange for them to cross paths with your spouse—either "accidentally" or purposefully, with a message from you. At each encounter, your enlisted accomplice should go out of his or her way to gush about your upcoming date—about how fun and relaxing it sounds and about how excited you are for it. If you know the right people at your spouse's place of employment, you might also persuade them to make an announcement about your date over a loudspeaker or in a company-wide memo.

MAKING IT WORK FOR YOU

Your first step is to schedule a date. It may be something big or extravagant, but it doesn't have to be, as long as it's something the two of you will look forward to. Once the date is scheduled, the two of you can start your campaign to build anticipation for it.

The obvious first step is personal communication—carefully worded tweets, texts, emails, and calls that express your own excitement and attempt to build your spouse's excitement for it. Chances are, you know just what to say to your spouse in order to make things more interesting. Here's your chance to say it in as many different ways as you can think of.

Your hype attempts may involve anything from chocolates to flowers to singing telegrams. You might write a message in chalk on your porch or build a snowman and have it hold a sign. Have fun with this. Let your imagination run wild as you let your spouse know how much you're looking forward to your date.

Obviously, you run the risk of building expectations so high that the actual date is a letdown. Do your best not to let that happen. But even if it does, that's okay. If you have enough fun with the buildup, that's the memory you and your spouse will take away from the adventure.

 ## SPEAKING THE RIGHT LANGUAGE

If Physical Touch is your spouse's primary love language, be sure you incorporate plenty of it into your buildup for your date. Something as simple as a quick massage of his shoulders or a gentle whisper in her ear can go a long way toward building anticipation.

WEAVING THE THIRD STRAND

Read together Matthew 24:36–51. In the passage, Jesus talks about His return. He builds anticipation for the event by pointing out that no one—not even the angels in heaven—knows when it will happen. He urges those who serve Him not to sit around and wait for Him to come back. Instead, He instructs us to stay busy doing His work.

Use the following questions as needed to guide your discussion of the passage. (Please note that the responses in parentheses are merely suggestions, ideas to stimulate your brainstorming and give you something to react to. They should not be viewed as the "correct" answers to the questions.)

▶ What do you take away from the fact that in Jesus' parable, the master gave his servants something to use while he was away? (Jesus has given each of us spiritual gifts—talents, abilities, interests, and skills—to put to use for His purposes.)

▶ Why did Jesus emphasize the importance of staying busy until He returns? (For one thing, there's a lot of work to be done. We are part of Christ's body in this world, doing His work and accomplishing His will. For another thing, it makes the anticipation and waiting easier.)

▶ How should we keep ourselves busy until Jesus' return? (Our primary responsibility is to lead others to Him, to share the good news that we were given. Beyond that, we have a responsibility to care for people in need, just as Jesus did.)

Pray together, thanking God for the assurance that Jesus will return. Ask Him to bless your efforts to stay busy and complete His work while you look forward to Jesus' second coming.

Suggested devotion from *The Love Languages Devotional Bible*, page 693 (Focusing on the Goal)

DOUBLE DATE: JUNIOR VERSION

THE END

Plan a double date with your parents—or with some other couple from an older generation. Enjoy one another's company and conversation while you learn from your older companions.

45

GOING THE EXTRA MILE

Plan an evening that resonates with your older companions. For example, you might dine at a restaurant where your fellow couple dined when they were dating. You might watch a classic movie together. You might have a picnic at one of their favorite spots—perhaps an arboretum or nature center. You might go to a museum that features items of interest to them. Plan your outing with an eye toward making your time together special for them.

MAKING IT WORK FOR YOU

Whatever you choose to do, your first priority should be to enjoy one another's company. If your double-date companions are your parents or your spouse's parents, this will give you an opportunity to interact as something close to peers. That may be a new dynamic for you or your spouse. If it is, embrace it. You may find that it has a profound effect on how you interact with your parents afterward.

Make conversation a priority throughout your adventure. Encourage your companions to share memories related to the places you go or the things you do. Obviously, you'll want to steer clear of sensitive issues or topics such as politics, which might inspire heated disagreement.

On the other hand, you might want to take the opportunity to ask questions to help you understand your parents better. Encourage them to talk candidly about the struggles they faced in their relationship and in raising a family. Pick their brains. Learn from their hard-earned lessons. Treat them like the mentors they are.

 ## SPEAKING THE RIGHT LANGUAGE

If your double date is with your spouse's parents— and if your spouse's primary love language is Words of Affirmation—you have a golden opportunity to make the evening special. Encourage your spouse's parents to share some parenting tips with you. Ask them to help you understand how they instilled such attractive qualities in your spouse. The more specific you can be about your spouse's attractive qualities, the more meaningful it will be—to your spouse and to the parents who raised him or her.

WEAVING THE THIRD STRAND

Read together Exodus 18:1–26. In the passage, Jethro, the priest of Midian and father-in-law of Moses, comes to visit Moses during the Israelites' journey to the promised land. He watches in bewilderment as Moses spends an entire day and evening serving as a judge, resolving the disputes of the Hebrew people.

Jethro encourages Moses to appoint judges to perform that task so he could save himself for the bigger responsibilities of leadership—though he would judge the really difficult cases. Moses followed Jethro's advice and learned to delegate. Thanks in no small part to Jethro's counsel, Moses became a great leader.

Use the following questions as needed to guide your discussion of the passage. (Please note that the responses in parentheses are merely suggestions, ideas to stimulate your brainstorming and give you something to react to. They should not be viewed as the "correct" answers to the questions.)

- ▶ What was Jethro's motivation for offering advice to Moses? (He wanted Moses to be the best leader he could possibly be—for Moses's own sake and for the sake of the people he was leading.)

- ▶ Why is it important to consider someone's motivation for offering advice before you act on that advice? (Sometimes people don't always have your best interests at heart.)

► Why is it important to maintain a spirit of humility? (Pride can fool you into thinking that you know more than you do. Humility encourages you to seek wisdom wherever you can find it.)

► Who do you usually turn to when you need advice that you can trust? (If your parents don't necessarily fit that bill, you may have a mentor or older sibling who does.)

► What's the best advice you've ever gotten? (For some people, it might be an investment tip. For others, it might be encouragement to pursue a certain career. For still others, it might be a heartfelt instruction to always put your spouse's needs ahead of your own.)

Pray together, thanking God for the sources of wisdom, instruction, and mentoring in your life. Ask Him to bless your efforts to become that kind of source in other people's lives.

Suggested devotion from *The Love Languages Devotional Bible*, page 81 (Taking Good Advice)

LEAVE IT TO THE KIDS

Here's an adventure you might consider a little risky. Let your kids decide what you're going to do. Give them the parameters of your date—how long you want it to last, how far you're willing to travel, and other basic information. Let them fill in the details. Commit yourselves to doing what your kids come up with.

46

GOING THE EXTRA MILE

If your kids are old enough to have social media accounts, take some time throughout your adventure to post updates in a private group chat with them. Let the planners of your date know how you enjoy each element they suggested. If you're feeling ambitious, you might even post photos. If you do, find ways to give credit to your kids in your captions. For example, you might take a picture of your wife on a dance floor and caption it with something like, "Thanks to you, your mom has found her inner Dancing Queen."

MAKING IT WORK FOR YOU

If your kids are young, they may need a little help in planning your date. You could give them options to choose from. For example, you might ask, "Should Mommy and Daddy go to a museum, take a long walk in the park, or go see a baseball game?" You could also give them options to choose from regarding where you'll eat during your adventure.

If your kids are older, encourage them to put some thought into their suggestions. Their ideas will likely be a mixture of things they like and things they assume you'll like. Ask them to share their reasons for suggesting certain things. In order to fully embrace this adventure, you'll need to be willing to step outside your comfort zone—at least a little. However, if your kids suggest something too far outside it, reserve the right to have them think of something else. Depending on how much control you're willing to surrender, you could even have them suggest topics of conversation for your date.

Whatever you and your kids decide on, do your best to carry it out, even if it feels a little awkward. When your adventure is over, spend some time debriefing with your planners. Be sure to thank them for their role in a memorable adventure.

SPEAKING THE RIGHT LANGUAGE

If your spouse's primary love language is Words of Affirmation, you can make this adventure special by talking about the positive qualities of him or her that you see in your children. Be specific in your praise and grateful in your demeanor for the fact that your kids have such a remarkable role model.

WEAVING THE THIRD STRAND

Read together 1 Timothy 4:12:

> "Don't let anyone look down on you because you are young, but set an example for the believers in speech, in conduct, in love, in faith and in purity."

Use the following questions as needed to guide your discussion of the passage. (Please note that the responses in parentheses are merely suggestions, ideas to stimulate your brainstorming and give you something to react to. They should not be viewed as the "correct" answers to the questions.)

- ▶ Why do people tend to underestimate or look down on young people—not just spiritually, but in other areas as well? (They mistake age for wisdom.)

- ▶ How would you describe your kids' spiritual maturity levels? If you have more than one child, assess each one individually. (Some kids may be mature in one area and lacking in another.)

- ▶ What do you see as the next step in your kids' spiritual maturity? (Depending on the age of your kids, you may see the next step as developing and maintaining a personal Bible study and prayer discipline, one that isn't dependent on your prompting.)

▶ What can you do to facilitate your kids' spiritual growth? (Perhaps the most important thing parents can do is to recognize their kids' individual spiritual journeys. Family devotions and prayer time are essential, but so is one-on-one conversation—talking with each child about his or her unique spiritual gifts, questions, doubts, and struggles.)

Pray together, thanking God for entrusting your children's spiritual grounding to you. Ask Him to bless your efforts to live an authentic Christian life that your children can learn from.

Suggested devotion from *The Love Languages Devotional Bible*, page 166
(The Truth about Consequences)

ON IMPULSE

47

What's the most impulsive thing you've ever done? Here's a chance to top it. With your spouse as an accomplice, take a giant step outside your comfort zone and do something that you normally wouldn't do if you had time to think it over.

GOING THE EXTRA MILE

Though it may sound like an oxymoron, you can help facilitate an impulsive decision by doing a little preparation beforehand. For example, having a gallon of the right color of paint on hand makes it easier to impulsively decide to paint your bedroom. Likewise, researching local tattoo parlors and knowing exactly what kind of design you want makes it easier to impulsively decide to get inked.

MAKING IT WORK FOR YOU

The list of potentially impulsive things to do is long and varied. You could shave your head. You could get a tattoo. You could paint a room of your house. You could go skydiving. You could get in the car and drive without knowing exactly where you're going.

No one is suggesting that you ignore your good judgment or do something that you'll regret—only that you silence the voices of fear and embarrassment that keep you from stepping outside your comfort zone and doing something that you really want to do.

During your adventure, talk about the areas of your life in which you're comfortable being bold, whether it's your physical appearance, your political beliefs, or something else. Let that lead into a discussion of areas in which you're *not* as comfortable being bold. Depending on your personality, that might include anything from standing up to your boss to talking about your Christian faith with certain friends or family members.

SPEAKING THE RIGHT LANGUAGE

If Quality Time is the primary love language of your spouse, you can make a big impression on him or her with a simple scheduling decision. Find an appointment in your schedule that you can impulsively cancel or postpone. Instead, make plans to spend that time with your spouse doing something that both of you enjoy.

WEAVING THE THIRD STRAND

Read together the following passages:

▶ Proverbs 28:1: "The wicked flee though no one pursues, but the righteous are as bold as a lion."

- Acts 4:13: "When they saw the courage of Peter and John and realized that they were unschooled, ordinary men, they were astonished and they took note that these men had been with Jesus."

- Hebrews 13:6: "So we say with confidence, 'The Lord is my helper; I will not be afraid. What can mere mortals do to me?'"

Use the following questions as needed to guide your discussion of the passages. (Please note that the responses in parentheses are merely suggestions, ideas to stimulate your brainstorming and give you something to react to. They should not be viewed as the "correct" answers to the questions.)

- Why would righteous people be bolder than wicked people? (Righteous people speak and act on God's behalf. Anyone who does God's work has His support. Knowing that, we can be as bold as we need to be.)

- Why does the reverse sometimes seem to be true? Why does it seem that righteous people flee while wicked people boldly do their thing? (Like Peter on the water in Matthew 14:28–30, righteous people sometimes lose sight of the Source of our boldness.)

- Look at Acts 4:1–22. After Jesus returned to heaven, His disciples Peter and John were brought before the Sanhedrin, a council filled with some of the most educated and respected men in all of Israel. Why did it seem as though Peter and John were outmatched? (They were uneducated fishermen.)

- ▶ Why were they able to speak so boldly under the circumstances? (They weren't trying to get into a theological debate with the Sanhedrin. They were simply sharing what they had seen and heard from Jesus. It's hard for people to argue against personal experience.)

- ▶ How do people react when they see boldness in others? (Some people are drawn to confidence and boldness. Others criticize or find fault when they encounter people who seem too presumptuous or sure of themselves. Either way, boldness tends to get people's attention.)

- ▶ If people were to embrace the spirit of Hebrews 13:6, what might they do? (They might share their faith with people who intimidate them. They might speak up for someone who's being bullied.)

Pray together, praising God for all that He has given us to be bold about. Ask Him to bless your efforts to be bold in your Christian witness.

Suggested devotion from *The Love Languages Devotional Bible*, page 249 (Speaking of Faith)

BIRTHDAY GREETINGS

48

Here's an opportunity to kill two birds with one stone. You can have a memorable adventure with your spouse *and* save money on greeting cards by recording creative birthday greetings for your friends and loved ones.

GOING THE EXTRA MILE

You could make this adventure extra special by searching out celebrities (even minor ones) to help you send birthday greetings. Depending on where you live, you may be able to find celebrities at charity events or promotional stops. With a little planning, you may be able to find local celebrities, newspeople, radio personalities, or athletes to help you record birthday greetings. If not, you could search out local celebrity impersonators and record some fun greetings with them.

MAKING IT WORK FOR YOU

All you need for this adventure is a phone with a video camera and a little creativity. Make a list of your friends and family members—the people you usually send birthday greetings to—and record a quick video message for each person that you can send on his or her birthday. Your messages may be funny, snarky, weird, or heartfelt, depending on the person.

You can have fun with this adventure by recording "out of season." That is, you might record a greeting for someone who has a summer birthday in winter—or vice versa. But you can make it seem as though you're recording it on the day of the birthday. For example, for someone with a mid-February birthday, you could stand out in the August sun and say, "Looks like you got some unusually warm weather for your birthday this year." Or, for someone with a summer birthday, you might start out with a close-up of a snowball. You could say, "You're probably wondering where we managed to find a snowball in the middle of August." Then you could pull back and show snow piled high everywhere and let the person try to figure out how you did it.

Store your video clips in an accessible file folder on your computer, with the names and dates clearly labeled, so you can upload them at the right time.

SPEAKING THE RIGHT LANGUAGE

If your spouse's primary love language is Physical Touch, script some of your birthday greetings accordingly. For example, in one clip, you might stage it as though you're wrestling for control of the camera. In another, you might stage it so that one of you is carrying the other.

WEAVING THE THIRD STRAND

Read together the following passages:

▶ Ecclesiastes 3:1–4: "There is a time for everything, and a season for every activity under the heavens: a time to be born and a time to die, a time to plant and a time to uproot, a time to kill and a time to heal, a time to tear down and a time to build, a time to weep and a time to laugh, a time to mourn and a time to dance."

▶ Psalm 118:24: "The LORD has done it this very day; let us rejoice today and be glad."

Use the following questions as needed to guide your discussion of the passages. (Please note that the responses in parentheses are merely suggestions, ideas to stimulate your brainstorming and give you something to react to. They should not be viewed as the "correct" answers to the questions.)

▶ Why do we celebrate birthdays—or "a time to be born," as the writer of Ecclesiastes puts it? (Birthday celebrations give us a chance to feel special, singled out, once a year. With social media, we may get greetings from people from several different periods of our lives. That offers a unique opportunity to reflect on how many people have influenced our lives—and on how many people have been affected by us.)

▶ Why is it important to take time to laugh and time to dance? (The pressures of family, work, finances, medical issues, and a host of other things can monopolize our time and attention, if we're not careful. That's why it's important to set aside time specifically to enjoy ourselves.)

▶ What's an appropriate way to celebrate, rejoice, and be glad for the blessings that God gives us every day? (Singing and giving praise to God through prayer are great ways to start. Maintaining a lighthearted spirit of gratitude and excitement, even in the face of difficulties, is another way.)

Pray together, thanking God for the seasons of life that make our lives rich and fulfilling. Ask Him to give you the wisdom to recognize and embrace each season as it comes.

Suggested devotion from *The Love Languages Devotional Bible*, page 668 (The Cup Is Always Half . . .)

IMPROMPTU GAMES

How creative are you? How competitive are you? Here's an opportunity to combine creativity and competitiveness for a memorable adventure with your spouse. Over the course of a few hours, see how many games you can make up, using just your imagination and any items you have on hand.

49

GOING THE EXTRA MILE

After you've played a few impromptu games, put your heads together and see if you can create a full-fledged game that your entire family can play. (You can play something like selfie hot potato. Pass a smartphone around after starting its timer function in the camera app. If it flashes while you are holding it, not only is there a silly photo of you, but you also have some sort of silly challenge to complete that is determined by the others.)

You'll need to consider the big picture—the object of the game—as well as the little details. You'll need to decide what is and isn't allowed in the game, what happens when a rule is violated, how to keep score, and how the game is ultimately won. Keep a list of the rules and regulations you come up with so you won't forget them. Who knows? You may create a new family favorite.

MAKING IT WORK FOR YOU

You can turn virtually anything into a game or competition. Case in point: if you have an ice cube, a pair of chopsticks, a kitchen counter, and something to use as goals, you can play a miniature hockey game.

You can also turn chores into competition. Let's say you're going to do your weekly grocery shopping. You have a list and you know that your weekly bill is usually right around $100. Here's what you do. You divide the list into two, with you and your spouse taking turns selecting items that each of you will buy. The person who spends closest to $50, buying only the items on his or her list, is the winner.

In the midst of your impromptu games, talk about how almost any situation can be made better—or, at least, more interesting—with a little creativity and thought. The key is being able to spot the potential for fun in any situation.

SPEAKING THE RIGHT LANGUAGE

If Quality Time is your spouse's primary love language, you can make this adventure special by creating a few games in which you and your spouse work together instead of competing against each other. For example, you might see how many paper wads the two of you can catch in a trash can in one minute. One of you will face away from the trash can and throw the paper wads over your shoulder as fast as you can. The other will run around with the trash can and try to catch the paper wads before they hit the ground.

WEAVING THE THIRD STRAND

Read together the following passages:

▶ 1 Corinthians 9:24: "Do you not know that in a race all the runners run, but only one gets the prize? Run in such a way as to get the prize."

▶ Philippians 2:3–4: "Do nothing out of selfish ambition or vain conceit. Rather, in humility value others above yourselves, not looking to your own interests but each of you to the interests of the others."

Use the following questions as needed to guide your discussion of the passages. (Please note that the responses in parentheses are merely suggestions, ideas to stimulate your brainstorming and give you something to react to. They should not be viewed as the "correct" answers to the questions.)

▶ The apostle Paul uses the analogy of a race that has only one winner in his discussion of the Christian life. What purpose does competitiveness serve? (Ideally, competitiveness can inspire us to give everything we have toward a pursuit—to use every bit of our God-given ability for His will.)

▶ When does competitiveness become a problem? (It becomes a problem when our desire to win—to prove ourselves "better" than other people—clouds our desire to give our best effort.)

▶ If we take Paul's words in Philippians 2:3–4 to heart, how might it affect our approach to competition? (We can still give our best effort in every pursuit. If, however, our best effort is bettered by someone else, we can be quick to celebrate with that person—to show graciousness and class when we don't win.)

Pray together, thanking God for equipping you to do His will in a competitive environment. Ask Him to bless your efforts to maintain a spirit of humility and consider the interests of others.

Suggested devotion from *The Love Languages Devotional Bible*, page 723 (Helpmate and Coworker)

DOUBLE DATE: SENIOR VERSION

Here's an adventure that will give you a chance to see your child in a different light—and give your child a chance to see you and your spouse in a different light. Plan a double date with your spouse, your child, and your child's date (a friend or someone your child is dating).

50

GOING THE EXTRA MILE

You can put your child's date at ease and avoid awkward conversational lapses by doing a little predate investigation. Find out as much as you can about your child's date, including his or her background, experiences, interests, and future plans. Work up some questions and discussion starters based on what you find out.

MAKING IT WORK FOR YOU

Your first and most obvious double-date option is to go out for dinner. If you don't know your child's date

very well, you may want to
opt for casual dining—pizza,
perhaps—so that everyone
feels at ease. Be prepared to
do much of the "heavy lifting"
when it comes to conversation—at least, at first. As much
as possible, try to strike a con-

versational balance between sharing your own thoughts and
stories and drawing out your child and his or her date. Resist
the urge to tease or embarrass your child, even if it seems like
harmless fun.

Continuing the casual theme, you might also play miniature golf or go bowling. That allows you to be together but
gives you something to focus on. It also creates an opportunity
for some good-natured competition.

SPEAKING THE RIGHT LANGUAGE

If Physical Touch is the primary love language of
your spouse, you can make this adventure special
for him or her—and instructive to your child.
You and your spouse can demonstrate affectionate and appropriate physical touch by holding hands and putting your arms
around each other throughout your date.

WEAVING THE THIRD STRAND

Read the following passages together:

► Psalm 71:17–18: "Since my youth, God, you have
taught me, and to this day I declare your marvelous

deeds. Even when I am old and gray, do not forsake me, my God, till I declare your power to the next generation, your mighty acts to all who are to come."

► Proverbs 9:9: "Instruct the wise and they will be wiser still; teach the righteous and they will add to their learning."

Use the following questions as needed to guide your discussion of the passages. (Please note that the responses in parentheses are merely suggestions, ideas to stimulate your brainstorming and give you something to react to. They should not be viewed as the "correct" answers to the questions.)

► What are the most important things that you learned from your parents? (Depending on what your parents were like, you may have learned anything from how to live a genuine Christian life to how to deal with bullies.)

► Why do you think God instructs young people to pay attention to the wisdom of older people? (Wisdom is hard-earned. Sometimes it can be gained only through life experience.)

► What's the connection between humility and wisdom? (Humility opens your mind to the possibility that you can learn a lot from other people—especially older people.)

► How can you help your kids benefit from your wisdom while you still maintain a spirit of humility? (One way is to resist the temptation to weigh in on every topic. If you express your opinion about everything or try to pretend that you have wisdom in an area when you really don't, you'll cheapen your words. If, however, you pick your moments to share your hard-earned wisdom, it likely will be better received.)

Pray together, thanking God for the opportunity to set an example for your kids. Ask Him to give you the wisdom, knowledge, and communication skills to prepare them for what lies ahead.

Suggested devotion from *The Love Languages Devotional Bible*, page 31
(Legacy of Lies)

TELL YOUR STORY

For the sake of future genealogists, make a video recording of yourself as you share everything you know about your roots. Talk about the stories of your ancestors that you were told by your parents and grandparents. Your goal is to help someone who's interested in researching your family tree fill in the branches.

51

GOING THE EXTRA MILE

If you're serious about getting the most from this adventure, do a DNA ancestry test beforehand. This will require some advance planning. Most DNA ancestry tests take several weeks to process.

The results usually include information about the makeup of your ancestry, with the different nationalities represented by percentages; the path of immigration your ancestors took, including the different places they settled; and the names of other people in the DNA ancestry database who may be related to you.

As you tell your story on camera, you can try to reconcile the results of your DNA ancestry test with what you were told about your family tree by your parents and grandparents.

MAKING IT WORK FOR YOU

Genealogy has become a very popular pastime. Even if no one in your family is currently passionate about tracing your family's roots, it doesn't mean that in the future someone close to you won't develop an interest in learning more about your ancestry. To assist future cultivators of your family tree, spend some time talking on camera about your family.

Accuracy counts, so you may want to use notes. Share as much vital information—full names, birth dates, birthplaces, hometowns, marriage dates, occupations, death dates—as you know. Fill in that information with your personal recollections of the people. Give your descendants a glimpse of what your loved ones were like.

SPEAKING THE RIGHT LANGUAGE

If your spouse's primary love language is Receiving Gifts, you can make this adventure special by having a professional genealogist dig into his or her ancestry. You may be surprised by what a professional can find. Obviously, you'll need to do some advance planning to pull this off. You can present the results to your spouse as part of your adventure.

WEAVING THE THIRD STRAND

Read together Galatians 3:26–29:

"So in Christ Jesus you are all children of God through faith, for all of you who were baptized into Christ have clothed yourselves with Christ. There is neither Jew nor Gentile, neither slave nor free, nor is there male and female, for you are all one in Christ Jesus. If you belong to Christ, then you are Abraham's seed, and heirs according to the promise."

Use the following questions as needed to guide your discussion of the passage. (Please note that the responses in parentheses are merely suggestions, ideas to stimulate your brainstorming and give you something to react to. They should not be viewed as the "correct" answers to the questions.)

- ▶ What connections do we have with people through our DNA and ancestry? (We're linked by common ancestors, the fact that two people in the distant past chose to procreate. We share a family history and perhaps some family resemblance, but that's about it.)

- ▶ How does that differ from the connections we have with people through Jesus Christ? (We have no choice in our ancestry. Through faith in Jesus, we join the body of Christ and become a part of the family of God.)

- ▶ What do Christians share in common? (We share a common experience. We've all had to acknowledge our sin, admit that we're helpless to save ourselves, and ask for God's forgiveness. We've all given our lives to Jesus. We all now work as His body on earth to accomplish His will.)

▶ Why don't racial and gender differences matter in the body of Christ? (We are all members of one body. Everyone has a job to do—a spiritual gift to put to use. That's what matters.)

▶ What should be our response to divisive issues? (On the one hand, we're called to speak the truth to one another in love. That may involve confronting a Christian brother or sister whose choices are causing harm to the body of Christ. But such confrontations should be done with a spirit of humility and love. Apart from that, we're called to seek unity with our fellow believers.)

Pray together, thanking God for the unity and fellowship we find in His family. Ask Him to give you the wisdom to know how to deal with potentially divisive issues.

Suggested devotion from *The Love Languages Devotional Bible*, page 1165 (No Favorites)

NAME THAT TUNE

This may be the most relaxing adventure in the book. You take a leisurely drive and listen to some of your favorite music from the past. You get nostalgic. If a song sparks a memory, you share it. You talk about what makes it special to you. What could be easier?

52

GOING THE EXTRA MILE

Instead of relying on a radio station programmer's playlist, create your own, using songs from when you and your spouse were young. You can do online searches for the top songs of certain years. That would be a good starting point. Don't confine yourself to your teenage years. Look for songs that were popular when you were very young. See if they inspire memories of listening to music with your parents—or perhaps even your grandparents. If you know there are certain songs that have special meaning to your spouse, include them.

MAKING IT WORK FOR YOU

Find the local oldies, classic rock, classic country, classic R & B, and/or classic hip-hop radio stations in your area. For this adventure, you might want to program them into your car's presets so you can find them easily.

When you hear a song that triggers a memory, talk about it. Is it a good or bad memory? Do you remember the song playing at the skating rink or swimming pool when you were young? Does it remind you of the summer your parents divorced?

If the radio doesn't cooperate, turn it off and take turns naming songs that carry powerful memories for you—perhaps the song that was playing when you had your first kiss or the song your grandmother used to sing to you. Let that lead into a discussion of why songs stir up memories.

SPEAKING THE RIGHT LANGUAGE

If your spouse's primary love language is Receiving Gifts, you can put a memorable cap on this adventure by presenting him or her with concert tickets to see one of his or her favorite performers. The two of you can then drive home, listening to the music of that performer.

WEAVING THE THIRD STRAND

Read together the following passages:

- ► Psalm 102:18: "Let this be written for a future generation, that a people not yet created may praise the LORD."

- ► Jeremiah 30:2: "This is what the LORD, the God of Israel, says: 'Write in a book all the words I have spoken to you.'"

Use the following questions as needed to guide your discussion of the passages. (Please note that the responses in parentheses are merely suggestions, ideas to stimulate your brainstorming and give you something to react to. They should not be viewed as the "correct" answers to the questions.)

- ► Are there any songs that remind you of something God has done for you? (If you can't think of any songs, expand the question a bit. Is there *anything* that reminds you of something God has done for you?)

- ► Why do you think God instructed the prophet Jeremiah to write down His words? (He wanted His people to remember and celebrate not just His words but also His actions—His miracles, His healings, His answers to prayer. If those things aren't written down, they may be forgotten. A similar principle applies to prayer journals.)

- ► What should we write down in our prayer journals? (One of the most helpful things you can do is to write the date of each entry, as well as a fairly detailed list of what you prayed for on that day. Be specific about the situations in which you ask God to intervene. What is it that you want accomplished? What specifically did you ask Him to do? After you've listed your prayer requests, make another list of answers to prayer that you've received. Over the long run, this will be the most important part of your journal because it allows you to trace God's work in your life.)

► What are the keys to effective journaling? (One key is to look carefully for answers to prayer that aren't so obvious. Just because God didn't do exactly what you wanted Him to do, exactly when you wanted Him to do it, doesn't mean that He didn't act on your request. Often, He works in and through specific situations in ways that can be seen only in retrospect. That's why it's important to keep careful records in your journal and to look back often at your previous requests.)

Pray together, praising God for His written Word. Praise Him also for specific things He's done in your life—things that deserve to be written down. Ask Him to bless your efforts to maintain a prayer journal that deepens your relationship with Him.

Suggested devotion from *The Love Languages Devotional Bible*, page 334
(Fresh Worship)

INDEX OF WAYS TO UNWIND
LOVE LANGUAGE FOCUS

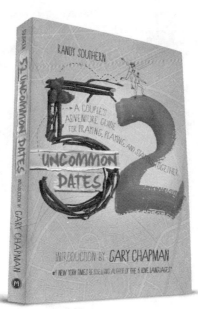

CONNECT WITH YOUR FAMILY
WITHOUT BREAKING THE BANK

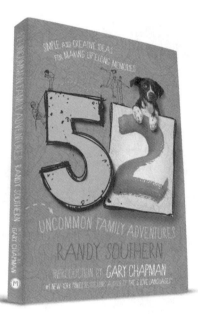

Whether it's a family pillow fight, a lip-sync competition, or Toilet Paper Olympics, give your family the gift of lifelong memories while having fun, connecting spiritually, and speaking each other's love languages. Enjoy all the benefits of the quality time you dreamed of without all the pressure of advanced planning.

978-0-8024-1939-2 | also available as an eBook

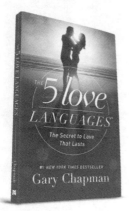

Improving millions of marriages...
one language at a time.

Discover the #1
New York Times bestseller
The 5 Love Languages®
by Gary Chapman

**The Love Languages
Devotional Bible**

Enjoy devotion
and intimacy on
so many levels.